Dearest

Elijah,

May God's wisdom guide you through all of life's situations. You are a great person.

Love & prayers,
Aunty Mary
[India]

500 FACTS

Ocean World

PEGASUS
www.pegasusforkids.com

© **B. Jain Publishers (P) Ltd.** All rights reserved. No part of this book may be reproduced, stored in a retrieval system or transmitted, in any form or by any means, mechanical, photocopying, recording or otherwise, without any prior written permission of the publisher.

Published by Kuldeep Jain for B. Jain Publishers (P) Ltd., D-157, Sector 63, Noida - 201307, U.P.
Registered office: 1921/10, Chuna Mandi, Paharganj, New Delhi-110055
Printed in India

CONTENTS

Preface 5

INTRODUCTION

Ocean Water 6

Ancient Oceans 10

Oceans Today 14

Oceans on the Move 22

Oceanic Division: Oceans of the World 26

Edge of the Ocean: Seas, Gulfs, Bays, Bights and Straits 34

Land Interaction: Rocky Shore, Ice Edge,
Fjord, Marsh, Estuary, Wetland and Coastal Forests 42

LIFE IN THE OCEANS

Plankton 54

Marine Mammals 57

Corals and Other Invertebrates 67

Celaphods, Crustaceans and Other Shellfish 80

Ocean Fishes 88

Sharks and Rays 94
Sea Turtles and Reptiles 100
Seabirds 104
Marine Algae and Plants 111

OCEAN ECOSYSTEMS

Coral Reefs... 121
Deep Hydrothermal Vents 130
Kelp Forests 138
Mangrove Forests 144
Seagrass Bed 155

UNDERSEA GEOLOGY

Seamounts, Underwater Earthquakes and Volcanoes 157

EXPLORING THE OCEAN

Incredible Technology 170

OCEAN LEGENDS

Mythology 177
Legends of the Ocean 180
Pirates and Famous Loot 184
Tragedies and Myths 189

PREFACE

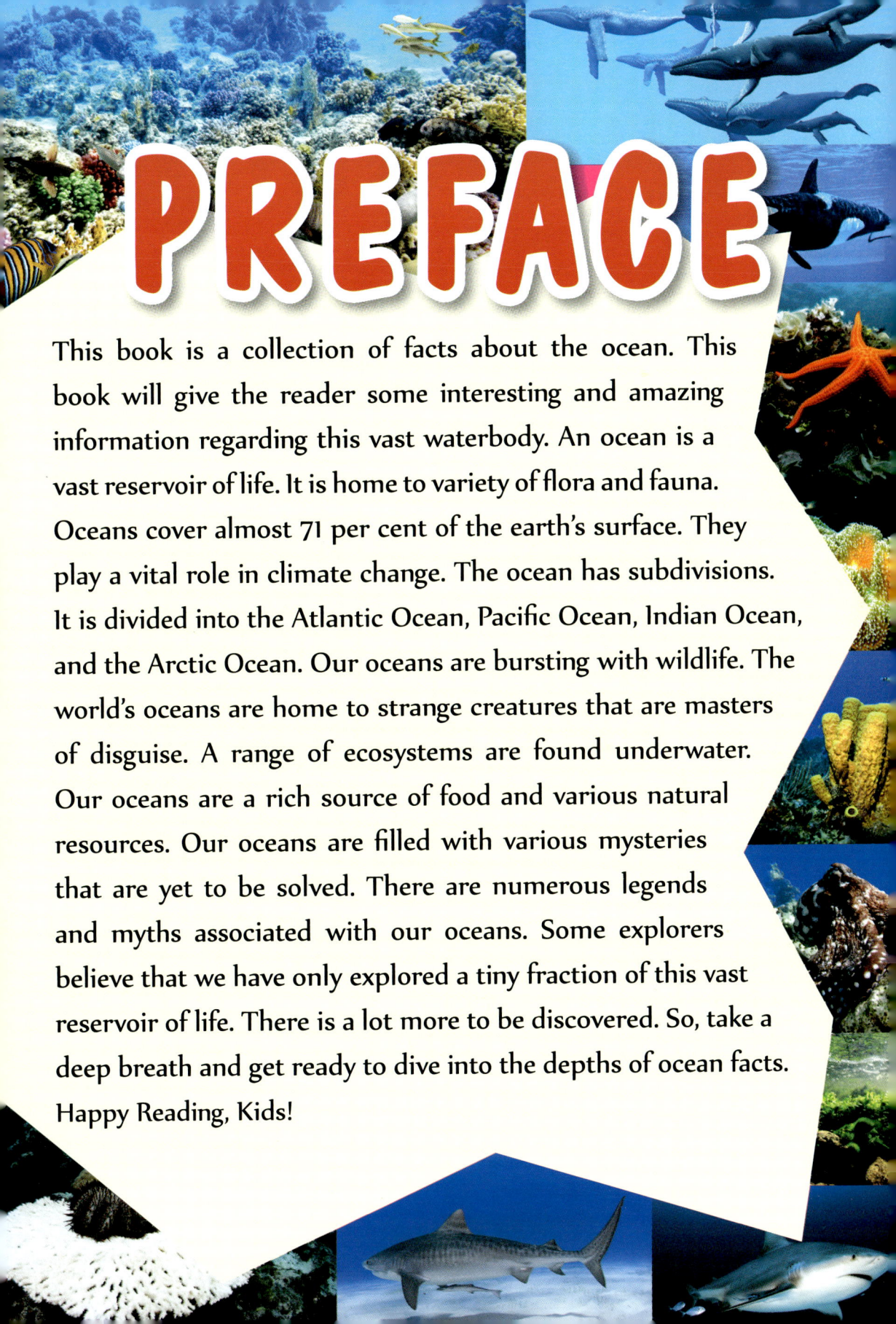

This book is a collection of facts about the ocean. This book will give the reader some interesting and amazing information regarding this vast waterbody. An ocean is a vast reservoir of life. It is home to variety of flora and fauna. Oceans cover almost 71 per cent of the earth's surface. They play a vital role in climate change. The ocean has subdivisions. It is divided into the Atlantic Ocean, Pacific Ocean, Indian Ocean, and the Arctic Ocean. Our oceans are bursting with wildlife. The world's oceans are home to strange creatures that are masters of disguise. A range of ecosystems are found underwater. Our oceans are a rich source of food and various natural resources. Our oceans are filled with various mysteries that are yet to be solved. There are numerous legends and myths associated with our oceans. Some explorers believe that we have only explored a tiny fraction of this vast reservoir of life. There is a lot more to be discovered. So, take a deep breath and get ready to dive into the depths of ocean facts. Happy Reading, Kids!

INTRODUCTION

Ocean Water

1 **Almost 71 per cent of the earth's surface is covered with oceans.** Together, the oceans contain 97 per cent of all the water on earth. This makes them essential for the survival of life on earth. Yet, we know very little about the oceans. Some explorers believe that we have explored less than five per cent of the oceans on earth!

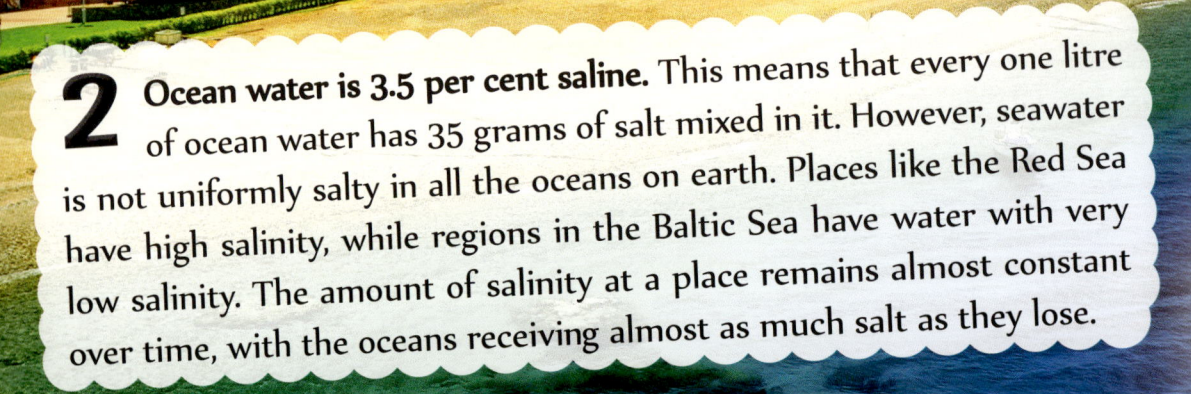

2 **Ocean water is 3.5 per cent saline.** This means that every one litre of ocean water has 35 grams of salt mixed in it. However, seawater is not uniformly salty in all the oceans on earth. Places like the Red Sea have high salinity, while regions in the Baltic Sea have water with very low salinity. The amount of salinity at a place remains almost constant over time, with the oceans receiving almost as much salt as they lose.

OCEAN WATER

3 **Do you know why seawater is salty?** The salt in oceans actually comes from the rocks on land. Rainfall and waves erode the rocks over time. This erosion results in the flow of particles called ions, which eventually flow into the oceans. Many of these ions are absorbed by sea creatures. Salt is formed by a combination of two of the unabsorbed ions: sodium and chloride.

4 There is another source of salt in the oceans. Its two constituents (sodium and chloride) are also derived from the ocean floor. Sodium is leached into the ocean during the process of ocean formation. Salt's other component, chloride, is formed during many of the ocean floor phenomena, like hydrothermal vents and volcanic eruptions.

5 **The salinity of seawater gives it a number of distinct physical properties.** The dissolved salt increases the mass in proportion to its volume, making the water denser than either pure water or freshwater. It also lowers its freezing point and raises its boiling point. Ocean water typically freezes at -2°C.

INTRODUCTION

Seawater contains many other elements.

6 **Apart from sodium and calcium, other commonly found ions are sulphate, magnesium, calcium and potassium.** Other chemicals found in seawater are carbon, strontium, boron, bromide and fluoride. Of these, magnesium and bromide are extracted for commercial use. In some places, seawater is still used for extracting salt.

7 **Seawater also contains many minor dissolved chemicals.** Of these, inorganic nitrogen and inorganic phosphorus are the most important, because these are essential for the survival of creatures that live in the sea. Many atmospheric gases such as carbon dioxide, oxygen and nitrogen are also found mixed in the seawater.

8 **Did you know that light behaves differently in oceans?** The refractive index of light can vary according to salinity and temperature of the water. Refractive index is the amount of refraction (or bending) of light in water. Much of the sunlight entering the water is refracted or absorbed, with very little light reaching the depths of the ocean.

OCEAN WATER

9 **If water is colourless, why does the ocean appear blue?** You may think it is because the ocean reflects the sky. But the reason is more complicated. The white light that enters the sea is composed of different wavelengths of red, yellow, orange and blue. The red, yellow and orange wavelengths are absorbed by the water, while the blue is scattered back.

10 **The sea may look calm, but it is a really noisy place.** Occasionally, there are explosions underwater, like volcanoes or earthquakes. Then, there is the chatter of sea mammals who often talk, moan and sing to each other! In addition, research shows that because of various human activities, like shipping, oceans are now 10 times more noisier than before.

11 **Since we cannot always look into the sea, sound is used to study the ocean.** Unlike sight, sound can travel over vast distances underwater. This is because water is an excellent conductor of sound, even better than air. However, sound behaves differently underwater than on the surface. Scientists use sound to locate and map the location of sea mammals.

Ancient Oceans

12 **The earth is at the right distance from the sun, for water to form on its surface.** About 4.5 billion years ago, the earth's temperature started to cool down from the furnace-like conditions at its origin. As the core formed, a number of gases escaped, forming a primitive atmosphere. The earth's atmosphere at this time was gaseous.

The formation of earth's core took about 500 million years.

13 **Even though oceans cover 71 per cent of the earth, these were not always a part of earth's surface in the same form as we know them.** It took many years for oceans to form on earth. But before that came water. Scientists are still unsure about exactly how water came on earth. Some believe that water came through comets, while some believe that the earth's rocks had water stored within, since the very beginning.

ANCIENT OCEANS

14 **As the temperature at the surface started to cool down, water vapour in the air began to condense and form clouds.** Then followed rains, that probably lasted for centuries. The rainwater drained and collected into basins on the earth's surface, forming vast oceans. The water reacted with other gases in the atmosphere and created the unique chemical composition of the oceans.

15 **It took billions of years to form the oceans.** In fact, the earth's surface is constantly changing even today. Changes in the ocean bed have changed the entire structure of the world, moving and removing continents and islands. The ancient earth looked nothing like today, with the oceans and continents distributed differently.

Map of the ancient earth

16 **The ancient oceans were starkly different.** Scientists believe that the oceans were considerably shallower during the last Ice Age, about two million years ago. The sea level was roughly 150 metres lower. This means that many regions covered by oceans today were dry land on the ancient earth. Land itself was not as fragmented by oceans as it is today.

11

INTRODUCTION

17 Roughly 200 million years ago, almost all of the earth's land mass was grouped together in one giant supercontinent called Pangaea. It was surrounded by a super ocean named Panthalassa. With time, Pangaea started splitting up, changing the very topography of the planet. As it broke down and the ocean replaced the breaks, Panthalassa too was divided into different water bodies.

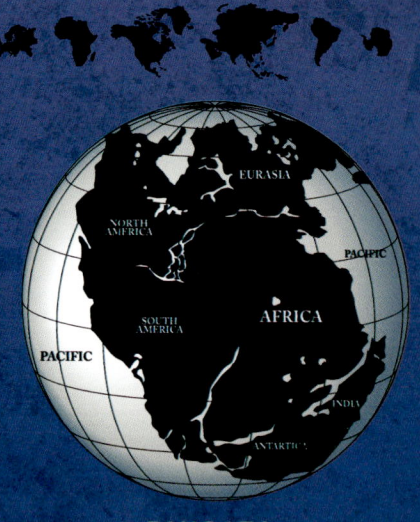

PANGAEA

18 Why does the ocean floor keep changing? The earth's surface, including the ocean floor, is made of large moving sections called plates. These plates are moving all the time, creating rifts and eruptions. Over a long period of time, they can slowly move the continents, changing the shape of land masses and oceans.

PLATE MOVEMENT

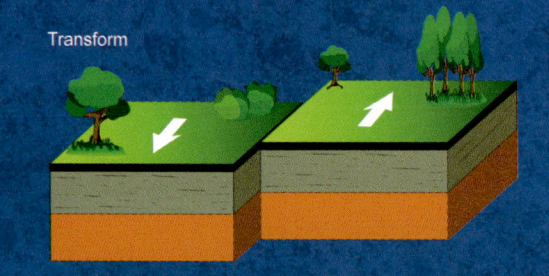

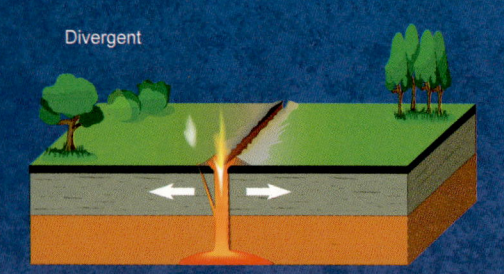

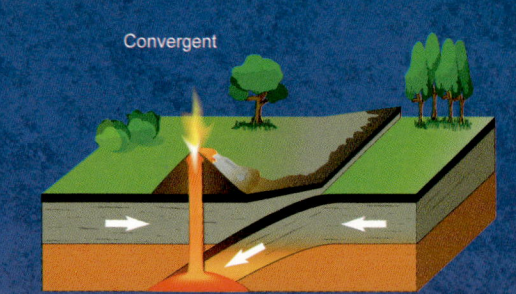

Transform

Divergent

Convergent

ANCIENT OCEANS

CONTINENTAL DRIFT

Pangaea | Laurasia and Gondwana | Modern World

19 Over time, Pangaea broke apart with one part drifting to the north and the other to the south. The part that drifted north was named Laurasia, while the southern part was called Gondwana or Gondwanaland. As the continents were drifting apart, magma from the earth's core came up to fill up the space and eventually became the floor of the Atlantic Ocean.

20 The ocean that replaced the space between Laurasia and Gondwana was named the **Tethys Ocean.** Eventually, Gondwana broke apart, opening up the Indian Ocean. As the continents continued to break apart, the spread of Tethys Ocean also changed, shrinking in some parts, while breaking apart and forming new oceans at other places.

Pangaea — PANGAEA 200 million years ago

Laurasia / Gondwana — LAURASIA & GONDWANA 120 million years ago

21 Over the years many oceans have disappeared due to climatic changes or plate movements. Even their chemical and mineralogical composition has changed as a result of various reactions on earth's surface and the climate. The modern oceans came into being roughly two billion years ago.

Oceans Today

22 **What goes into making our modern oceans?** What are its physical characteristics? To the naked eye, the ocean is just a vast reservoir of water. But as we have read before, the ocean also has many gases, minerals and chemicals. In addition, it is full of life, teeming with fishes, animals, plants and microscopic creatures.

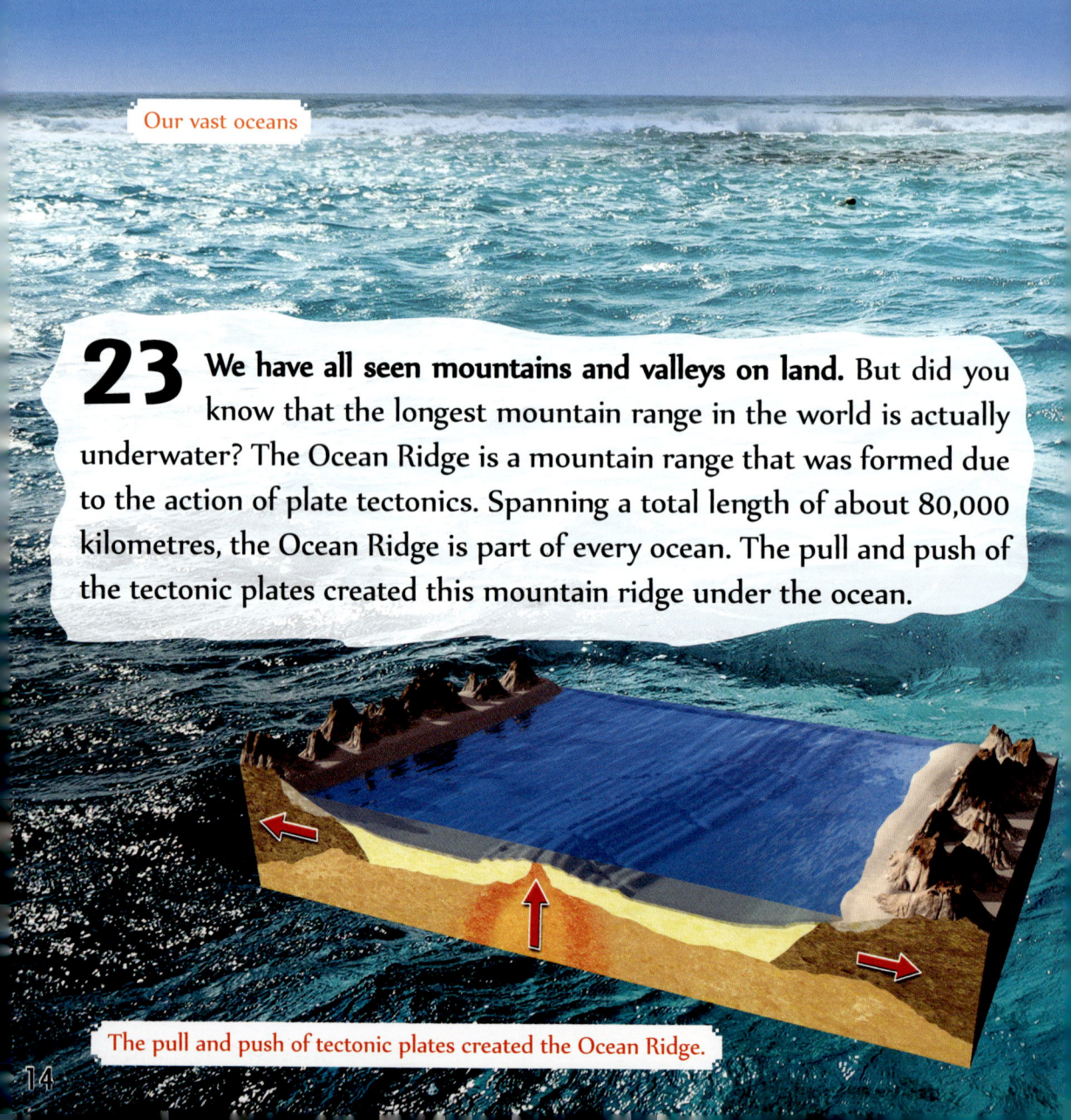

Our vast oceans

23 **We have all seen mountains and valleys on land.** But did you know that the longest mountain range in the world is actually underwater? The Ocean Ridge is a mountain range that was formed due to the action of plate tectonics. Spanning a total length of about 80,000 kilometres, the Ocean Ridge is part of every ocean. The pull and push of the tectonic plates created this mountain ridge under the ocean.

The pull and push of tectonic plates created the Ocean Ridge.

OCEANS TODAY

24 **The oceans are very vast and change drastically from place to place and even as we move up and down.** That is why oceanographers have divided oceans into different zones. So, there are two ways of dividing the ocean: horizontally, as we move from the seashore and vertically, as we go down to the seafloor.

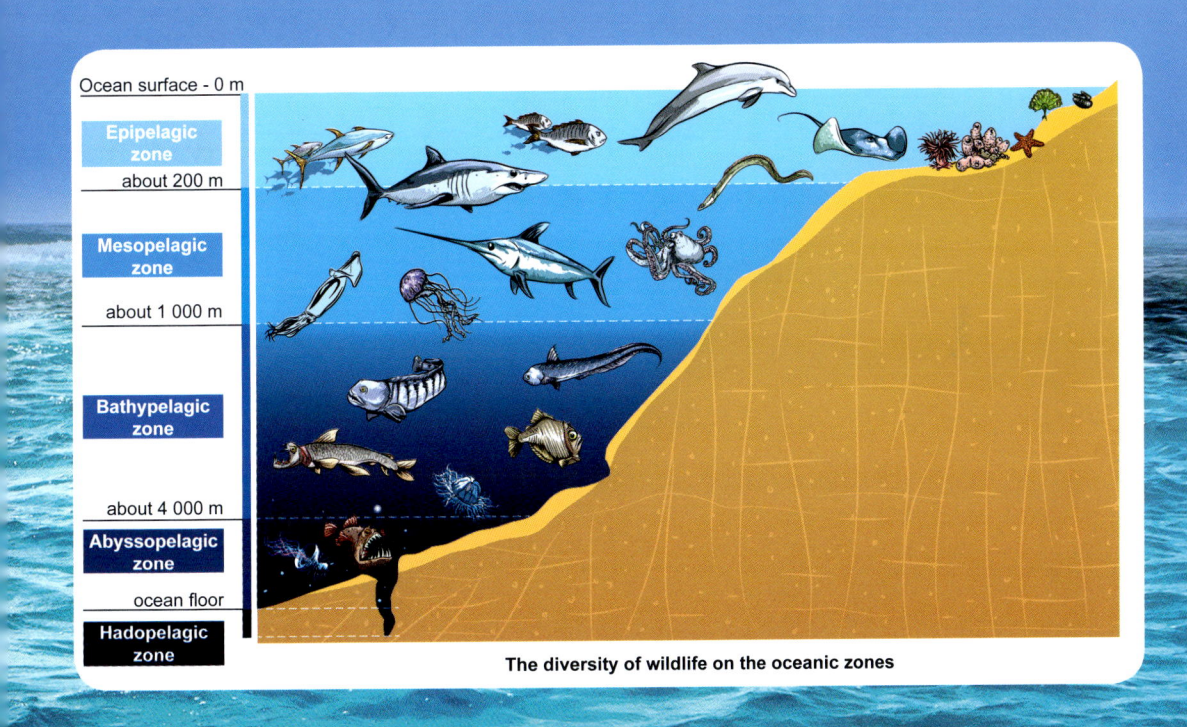

Ocean surface - 0 m
Epipelagic zone
about 200 m
Mesopelagic zone
about 1 000 m
Bathypelagic zone
about 4 000 m
Abyssopelagic zone
ocean floor
Hadopelagic zone

The diversity of wildlife on the oceanic zones

The zones were initially created to study animals

25 **The horizontal zone begins with the littoral zone, which includes the intertidal zone.** This is the area between high tide and low tide. It is submerged in water during high tide and then exposed to the air during low tide. The organisms found here must adapt to both extremes. It contains a wide variety of habitats like tide pools and inlets.

INTRODUCTION

26 The next zone is the pelagic zone, which starts from the low tide mark and includes the open ocean. In other words, almost the entire ocean comes under this zone. It is rich in life, but the abundance decreases with depth. The pelagic zone is divided into two subzones: neritic zone and oceanic zone.

27 The oceanic zone contains the largest mass of the ocean. It begins from the edge of the continental shelf and extends over the ocean beyond. It goes down to the depth of the ocean floor. This zone contains volcanoes, trenches, and ocean basins. It is further divided into vertical zones.

28 The water over the continental shelf comes under the neritic zone. The continental shelf is the edge of the continental mass that is always submerged in water. Sunlight and its closeness to land means that this zone is rich in nutrients and life. Habitats found here include kelp forests and coral reefs.

OCEANS TODAY

29 **The vertical division of the oceanic zone is based on the amount of sunlight penetration and the water pressures at different levels.** At the top is the sunlit zone because it is open to the sun and receives abundant sunlight. This is where photosynthesis takes place and we have abundant life with planktons, invertebrates and animals.

30 **Below the sunlit zone is the mesopelagic or twilight zone.** Even though it is just under the sunlit zone, it only receives faint, filtered light because most of the light is absorbed by the ocean above. It begins from about 50 feet to 600 feet depending on the murkiness of the water. The temperature remains fairly stable, but pressures can reach up to 1,470 psi (pound force per square inch).

INTRODUCTION

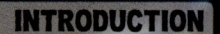

31 Till the mid-20th century, scientists dismissed the idea of animals living in the twilight zone because of the high pressure. But now we know that many animals actually thrive in these conditions. They are adapted to life in near-darkness, cold and high pressure. They are experts at camouflage and some are even bioluminescent.

Jellyfish, an inhabitant of the twilight zone

Octopus in the midnight zone

32 Under this is the bathypelagic zone, also called the midnight zone. It is named so because almost no light filters into this zone. Because of this, the water is almost freezing. As a consequence there is almost no photosynthesis. The organisms that live here include whales, frill sharks, squids and octopuses.

33 **The deepest layer of the ocean is the abyssal zone, ending in the seafloor.** It stretches from 13,000 feet to about 20,000 feet beneath the surface. There is no sunlight which penetrates this zone. Hence, it is under perpetual darkness and freezing cold. Added to this is the tremendous water pressure at the bottom of the sea!

Southern rock lobster

34 **The lack of sunlight and pressure may seem to create inhospitable conditions, but the abyssal zone actually has plenty of life.** Here we find deep trenches, fissures and hydrothermal vents. Bacteria and tube worms in the hydrothermal vents form food sources for other organisms.

35 **According to its density, the ocean is divided into three parts:** the surface zone, the pycnocline zone and the deep zone. The surface zone is usually defined between depths of 500 feet to 3,300 feet. The pycnocline zone is seen as the dividing line between the surface zone and the deep zone, which begins at 3,300 feet.

INTRODUCTION

36 **The surface zone, as the name suggests, is at the top of the ocean.** It is also called the mixed zone, as it sees action from many other factors like the wind. Since it receives direct sunlight, it is also the warmest zone. It is the least dense of all zones with a constant level of temperature and salinity. It contains roughly two per cent of the ocean's water.

37 **The pycnocline zone is the dividing line between the surface zone and the deep zone, effectively acting as a buffer between the two extreme densities.** This stable zone isolates the effect of these two distinct zones from each other. Within the zone, the density increases dramatically as we go down.

38 **The deep zone lies at the very bottom of the ocean.** Here the water is freezing cold. Both the temperature and salinity remains stable at this level. At this depth, the water is extremely dense. However, within this zone, there is very little change in density with depth. The deep zone contains roughly 80 per cent of the total volume of ocean water.

OCEANS TODAY

39 **The division of ocean layers is not just for our convenience.** The changes in temperature, salinity, pressure and density affect many aspects of our oceans. It determines the spread, variety and lifestyles of organisms found in different layers. It also affects the currents, which in turn affects weather patterns across the world.

40 **The oceans today cover about 71 per cent of the earth's surface.** Ocean water is saline with varying degrees of temperature, pressure and density. It is a habitat for more than 230,000 known species. Importantly, oceans are integral to life on the planet and act as a major influencing factor on climate and weather changes across the globe.

Oceans on the Move

41 **The ocean is never still, even when it may appear calm.** We can see this motion from the shores or from a ship, as waves travel through ocean waters. On the beach, you may have even seen information and warnings about currents. The ocean water is constantly moving from north to south, east to west, and vice versa.

42 **There are many factors that influence the movement of the ocean water.** Wind forces, water, gravity, salinity, density and temperature—all these factors can influence the motion of water on the surface as well as under it. Broadly speaking, this motion is seen in three ways: waves, tides and ocean currents.

43 **Ocean waves are affected greatly by the wind.** They are created by the transfer of energy from the wind to the water, which results in a horizontal movement in the water. Waves may seem like ripples with a vertical movement, but each particle of water is actually moving in a completely circular motion under the surface.

44 **Like any other wave, an ocean wave also has two major parts: a crest and a trough.** The raised part is called the crest, while the dip in between two waves is the trough. Waves are measured according to their wavelength or their amplitude. The wavelength is the distance between crests, while amplitude is the measurement from crest to trough.

45 **Waves collapse when they hit the shore.** This is because the wave's energy is transferred to the shore. Sometimes, waves are also created by underwater landslides or earthquakes. The resultant waves start out very small in the deep ocean. But as they reach the land, the wave height increases. The height and energy of such waves is immense.

INTRODUCTION

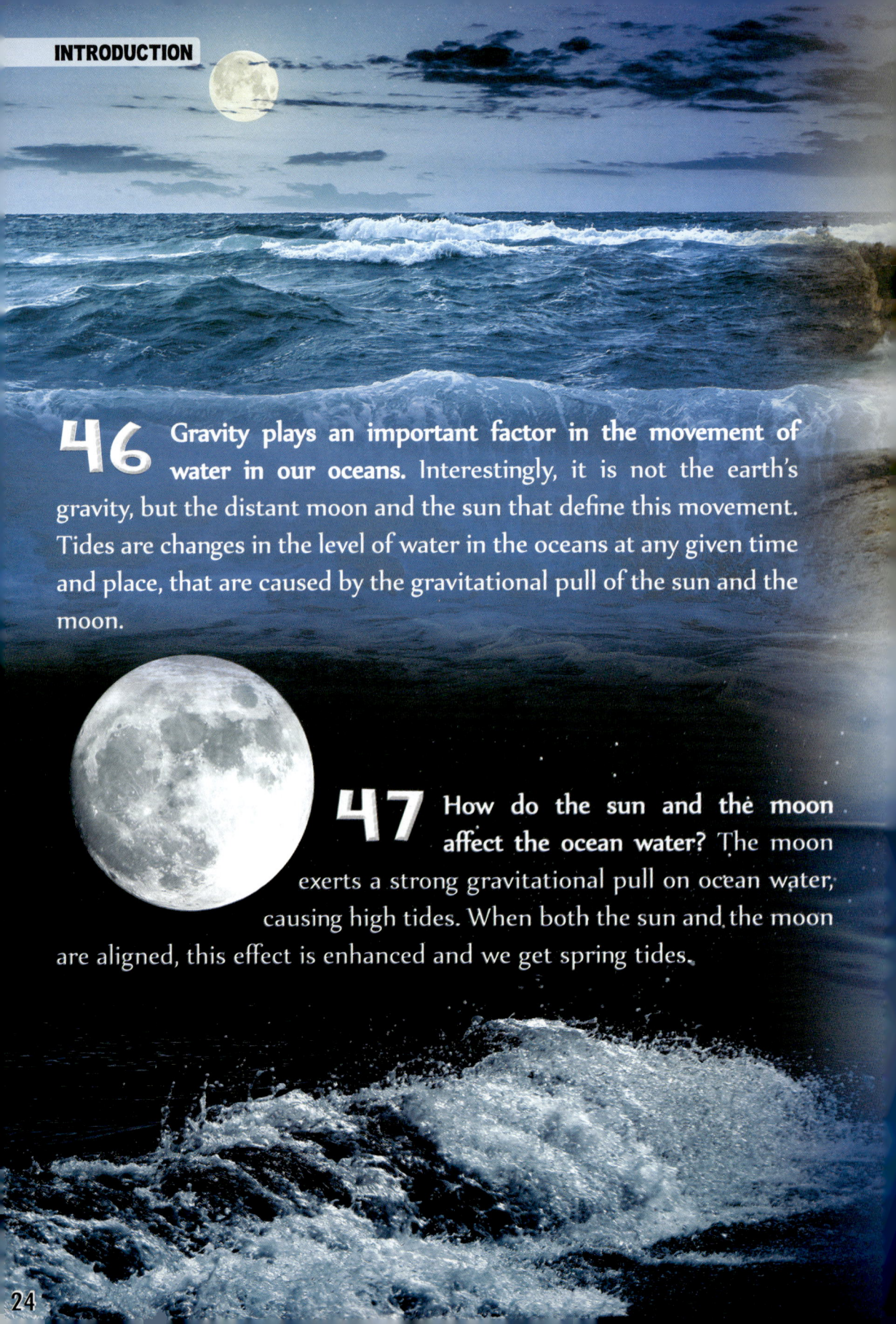

46 **Gravity plays an important factor in the movement of water in our oceans.** Interestingly, it is not the earth's gravity, but the distant moon and the sun that define this movement. Tides are changes in the level of water in the oceans at any given time and place, that are caused by the gravitational pull of the sun and the moon.

47 **How do the sun and the moon affect the ocean water?** The moon exerts a strong gravitational pull on ocean water, causing high tides. When both the sun and the moon are aligned, this effect is enhanced and we get spring tides.

OCEANS ON THE MOVE

48 An ocean current is the large movement of water in one direction for a great distance. They can be temporary or last over a long period of time. Large currents that last over a long time decide climate patterns around the earth, as they carry heat. The flow of currents is influenced by wind patterns, earth's rotation, temperature and salinity.

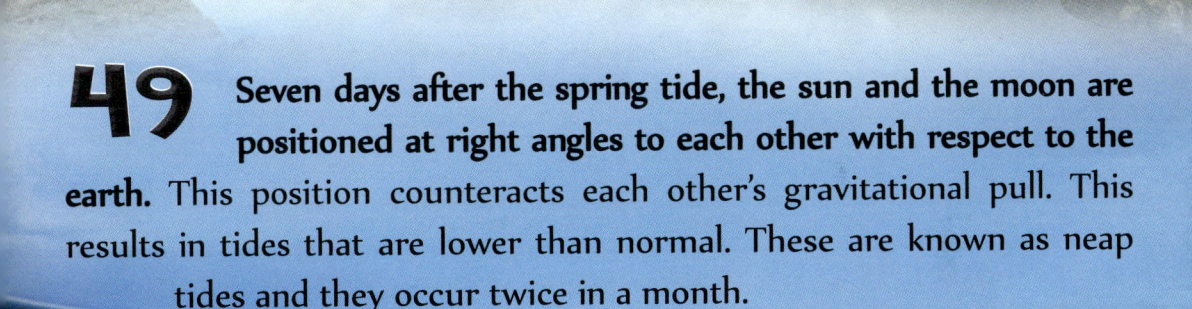

49 Seven days after the spring tide, the sun and the moon are positioned at right angles to each other with respect to the earth. This position counteracts each other's gravitational pull. This results in tides that are lower than normal. These are known as neap tides and they occur twice in a month.

50 There are currents deep within the oceans as well, and these are called deep currents. Like the surface currents, deep currents keep moving the water underneath the ocean's surface. These are influenced by salinity and temperature. Salinity and low temperature raises the water density. As the dense water sinks, lighter water rushes to fill the surface at the top. Thus, it causes movement of water.

Oceanic Division: Oceans of the World

51 **There is actually one World Ocean or one body of water that covers most of our planet.** We have divided this ocean for historical, geographical or scientific reasons into five oceans. These are Atlantic, Pacific, Indian, Arctic and Antarctic (Southern) Oceans. Of these the Atlantic, Pacific and Indian Oceans are recognised as the major oceans of the world.

52 **The Pacific Ocean is the largest and deepest ocean in the world.** It extends from the Arctic Ocean in the north, Antarctic Ocean in the south, Asia and Australia in the west and the Americas in the east. In area it measures about 63.8 million square miles. The deepest point on earth, Mariana Trench with a depth of 10,911 metres, also lies in the Pacific.

53 **The Pacific Ocean is among the oldest of the modern oceans.** It originated from the Panthalassa Ocean that encompassed the supercontinent Pangaea. Scientists believe that the ocean was formed soon after the breaking up of Pangaea about 250 million years ago, even though the oldest known ocean floor in the Pacific is about 180 million years old.

The Pacific Ocean originated from the Panthalassa Ocean that surrounded the supercontinent Pangaea.

OCEANIC DIVISION: OCEANS OF THE WORLD

54 **The word 'Pacific' comes from the Latin word 'pace' which means peace.** It was named by a Portuguese explorer Ferdinand Magellan, who claimed that the sea was 'mar pacifico', meaning peaceful sea. However, the ocean is not really as peaceful as it appears. In fact, it is home to 75 per cent of the earth's volcanoes. It also sees frequent tsunamis and earthquakes.

55 **The equator divides the Pacific Ocean into two parts—the North Pacific Ocean and South Pacific Ocean.** The Pacific is home to many islands and archipelagos. The world's largest coral reef—the Great Barrier Reef—also lies in the Pacific. Due to the movement of the earth's plates, the Pacific is slowly shrinking, while the Atlantic Ocean is growing.

Ariel view of the Great Barrier Reef

INTRODUCTION

56 With its vast expanse, the Pacific Ocean has the ability to influence the climate of the entire planet. Whenever warm currents form in the Southern Pacific, temperatures go up in coastal areas of Chile and Ecuador. This can, in turn, trigger severe weather conditions in the rest of the world, from floods to typhoons!

57 The Atlantic Ocean is the second largest ocean on the earth. It covers roughly 20 per cent of the planet's surface with a total area of approximately 106,460,000 square kilometres. It is an elongated S-shaped basin between the Americas and the continents of Europe and Africa.

58 The word 'Atlantic' comes from the Greek mythological figure, Atlas. It means 'sea of Atlas'. However, the ancient Greeks referred to the Atlantic as Oceanus. It was seen as a gigantic river that covered the world. The equator divides it into the North Atlantic Ocean and South Atlantic Ocean.

OCEANIC DIVISION: OCEANS OF THE WORLD

View of the Straits of Gibraltar

59 **Because of its location, the Atlantic Ocean has played an important role in the transportation of people.** Important waterways of the Atlantic include the Straits of Gibraltar, between Morocco and Spain and the Bosporus in Turkey. It was named the black Atlantic because of its role in the transportation of slaves during the early modern period.

60 **Scientists believe that the Atlantic Ocean was formed 180 million years ago when the supercontinent Pangaea broke up.** The break resulted in the formation of the eastern and western hemispheres, opening up the Atlantic Ocean basin. It also resulted in the Mid-Atlantic Ridge—an underwater volcanic zone with mountains and faulted plateaus.

INTRODUCTION

61 The Indian Ocean is the third largest ocean on the earth, covering roughly 70,560,000 square kilometres. It accounts for 20 per cent of the planet's water. It lies between Asia in the north, Africa in the west, Australia in the east and the Antarctic Ocean in the south. There is still some dispute over its borders. Till recently, it was thought to also include some parts of the Antarctic Ocean.

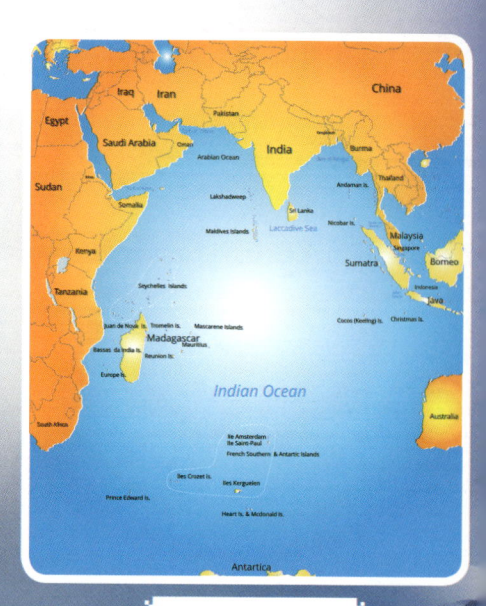

The Indian Ocean

62 The Indian Ocean gets its name from India. In ancient Sanskrit literature, it is also called the Hind Mahasagar. A worldwide oceanic ridge of seismically active mountain chains passes through the Indian Ocean. This ridge is also the centre of the spreading seafloor in some places.

OCEANIC DIVISION: OCEANS OF THE WORLD

63 **The Indian Ocean is the youngest of the major oceans.** It was formed after the breakup of the supercontinent Gondwanaland in the southern hemisphere. As the division rearranged the continents, the Indian Ocean came into existence about 140 million years ago. This creation took time and most of the ocean is thought to be less than 80 million years old.

The Arctic Ocean

64 **With its location in the North Pole, the Arctic Ocean is influenced by the polar climate.** Parts of it are covered throughout the year with sea ice. In winter, the ocean is almost completely covered with ice. The polar conditions also affect the salinity of the ocean. The average salinity of the Arctic Ocean is the lowest among the five oceans.

65 **The Arctic Ocean is the smallest and shallowest ocean in the world.** In fact, it is often referred to as a sea. It is the northernmost part of the world ocean, falling mostly in the North Pole. The Arctic Ocean is almost completely surrounded by North America and Eurasia. Because of its remoteness, it is one of the least explored oceans.

INTRODUCTION

66 **Did you know that the Arctic ice packs are almost always on the move?** The rising global temperature has had a considerable effect on these ice floes. The polar ice cap is slowly shrinking each year and experts predict that by the year 2040, Arctic Ocean may become completely free of ice.

67 **Also known as the Southern Ocean, the Antarctic Ocean is the most recently named ocean.** It is the fourth largest ocean, larger only than the Arctic Ocean. Falling in the South Polar region, the ocean encircles the continent of Antarctica. This also makes it the southernmost spread of the one World Ocean.

68 **Like the Arctic Ocean, the Antarctic Ocean is also influenced by polar climatic conditions.** Icebergs are found in the ocean at any time of the year. From May to October, strong winds blow which makes navigating the water difficult.

OCEANIC DIVISION: OCEANS OF THE WORLD

69 **The Antarctic Ocean is considered to be the youngest ocean.** It was formed only 30 million years ago when Antarctica separated from South America as a result of tectonic plate movements. This separation of plates opened up the Drake Passage, which in turn allowed a water current to form around the Antarctic. This was the Antarctic Circumpolar Current.

70 **It was in the 1770s that Captain James Cook had declared that the ocean waters surrounded the southern part of the globe.** Even though the oceanic waters have been divided into five parts, it is important to remember that it is one single waterbody. This is especially important when studying the ocean currents, or life forms within the waters.

Edge of the Ocean: Seas, Gulfs, Bays, Bights and Straits

71 **If we see the World Ocean as one ocean, then its borders lie with continents, islands and archipelagos.** But the edge of the ocean where it meets land are often described as seas, gulfs, bays, bights, and straits. The classification is merely according to its interaction with the land and the way the waterbody is shaped when it meets land.

72 **Although the terms sea and ocean are often used interchangeably, there are some definite differences.** Oceans are vast and interconnected to become one enormous World Ocean. On the other hand, a sea lies at its edge. It is a much smaller part of the ocean that is partially enclosed by land.

EDGE OF THE OCEAN: SEAS, GULFS, BAYS, BIGHTS AND STRAITS

73 Since the sea is essentially a part of the ocean, its physical characteristics remain the same. It is a saline body of water surrounded partially by land. It plays an important role in the earth's ecosystem—from influencing weather to the water cycle, nitrogen cycle and carbon cycle.

The sea is surrounded partially by land.

74 The seas are divided according to the oceans—Atlantic, Pacific, Indian, Arctic and the Southern or Antarctic Ocean. With their proximity to land and shallow continental shelves, the seas are full of nutrients, sustaining a rich ecosystem. Hence, the sea is a rich source of food for humans and many portions of the sea are used for human benefit.

75 Depending on their formation, there are three basic types of seas: partly enclosed seas, nearly enclosed seas and hypersaline lakes. Partly enclosed seas are hemmed by land and open to the ocean. Nearly enclosed seas are almost landlocked with just a narrow waterway connecting to the ocean. Hypersaline lakes were part of ancient oceans, which are now landlocked.

INTRODUCTION

76 Nearly enclosed seas are almost landlocked. These are connected with the ocean through narrow waterways called 'straits'. With such a narrow connection, there are very few similarities in the chemical, physical or biological make-up of the two kinds of waterbodies. Some seas may not even experience any tides. Examples include the Baltic Sea and Mediterranean Sea.

The Baltic Sea

77 The Red Sea, located between Africa and Asia, is connected to the Indian Ocean through the Bab-el-Mandeb strait and the Gulf of Aden. It is far more saline than the ocean. As a consequence, its inhabitants have adapted to its conditions and these creatures are not found in the ocean!

The Red Sea

EDGE OF THE OCEAN: SEAS, GULFS, BAYS, BIGHTS AND STRAITS

78 Partly enclosed seas are more influenced by the ocean since they are only partially hemmed by land, such as islands, peninsulas or archipelagos. Because of this, their essential characteristics remain largely the same as the ocean. For instance, the organisms found in these seas are seen in the ocean as well.

Salty deposits at the shore of the Dead Sea.

79 Some waterbodies are called seas because of their high salinity, but they are actually lakes. These were once part of the ocean, but later tectonic shifts and the process of deposition over time blocked their connection with the ocean. These are now completely landlocked. Some of these are highly saline and are known as hypersaline lakes, such as the Dead Sea.

The Caspian Sea

80 The Caspian Sea, landlocked between Europe and Asia, is an interesting example of a hypersaline lake, which also contains freshwater in its northern portion. The Dead Sea, on the other hand, is an excellent example of a true hypersaline lake. It is almost 10 times saltier than the ocean and hence, contains almost no life!

INTRODUCTION

81 **Other waterbodies that border oceans are bays, gulfs and straits.** These are located near land, forming a connection between the land and the ocean. This also makes them important centres for human activity, such as for trade in maritime goods. These bodies sometimes also become part of conflict over territory.

82 **A bay is a recessed body of water, usually formed in coastal regions where the land curves inward.** They are connected to the larger body of water on one side. Bays have played an important part in human settlement in coastal regions. They provide an ideal nook for fishing and maritime trade.

A view of islands in Halong Bay, Vietnam.

EDGE OF THE OCEAN: SEAS, GULFS, BAYS, BIGHTS AND STRAITS

83 **Bays are usually formed because of plate tectonics.** As the continents broke up, the land curved inwards or fissures resulted, which were filled up by the surrounding ocean. These became the bays. Bays are also found inland, near oceans, lakes and even, in some cases, rivers. Some examples of bays are James Bay, Hudson Bay and the Bay of Bengal.

84 **The Bay of Bengal is the largest bay in the world, covering an area of 2,172,000 square kilometres.** Part of the Indian Ocean, it has an almost triangular edge against the Indian peninsula. A number of major rivers drain into the bay, depositing rich sediments. The bay has a rich biological diversity, counted among the world's richest ecosystems.

85 **A gulf is often taken as a bigger version of a bay. However, it is also deeper and larger with a narrow opening.** This means that a gulf is almost landlocked. Their formation, like bays, was due to plate tectonics, when part of the ocean was trapped in the rising landmass. Examples of gulfs are the Persian Gulf, Gulf of Aden and Gulf of Mexico.

INTRODUCTION

86 **The Gulf of Mexico is the largest gulf in the world.** It is surrounded by the North American continent. It has an oval-shaped basin, connected to the Atlantic Ocean through the Florida Straits. Geologists believe that this area was once all land. The rifts and collisions of continental plates caused a thinning of the crust, which then got flooded with ocean water.

87 **A strait is narrow channel between two landmasses that connects two larger bodies of water.** Straits are usually navigable unless they are too shallow. A strait is also sometimes known as a channel or passage. Since they form an important gateway to harbours, straits were historically highly valued, with wars fought over their control!

Aerial photograph of the Gulf of Mexico.

88 **One of the most important and sought after straits is the Strait of Gibraltar.** Separating Gibraltar and peninsular Spain from Morocco and Ceuta, it connects the Mediterranean Sea with the Atlantic Ocean. The strait ensures flow of water between the two oceans, helping in maintaining their stability and salinity.

EDGE OF THE OCEAN: SEAS, GULFS, BAYS, BIGHTS AND STRAITS

89 A 'bight' is a bend or recess in the shoreline which begins gradually and forms an open bay. These are typically quite shallow. Many bights also have features like sand bars and rock formations at their basin. This makes navigation difficult. Traditionally, bights were seen as tricky passages, with their features carefully marked on navigation maps.

Cliff Coastline, Western Australia

90 One of the most important bights in the world is the Great Australian Bight. It lies off the central and western portions of the southern coastline of mainland Australia. The bight has many cliffs and beaches. It is an important migratory platform, especially for southern right whales which come here for breeding.

The Great Australian Bight

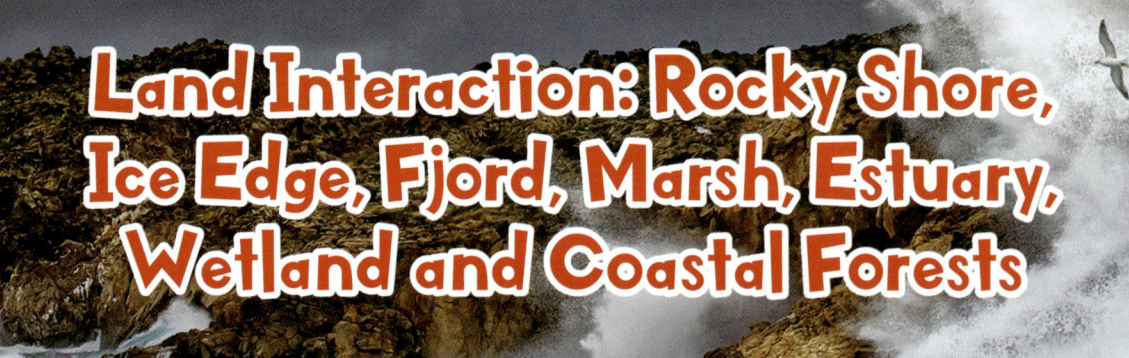

Land Interaction: Rocky Shore, Ice Edge, Fjord, Marsh, Estuary, Wetland and Coastal Forests

91 While oceans were changed because of continental drifts and motions, the oceans in turn have a profound effect on land, especially on its coastline. As the waves batter against the coast, it changes its shape and character. This slow process has determined the shape of our coastlines and, by effect, the continents.

92 The coastal environment represents the transition from land to ocean. This is a very complex ecosystem where many factors come into play. Along the coastline, there are several points of confluence where rivers from the continents drain into the ocean. At these points, erosion, sediment deposition, waves interaction take place.

LAND INTERACTION: ROCKY SHORE, ICE EDGE, FJORD, MARSH, ESTUARY, WETLAND AND COASTAL FORESTS

93 The factors that determine the ecology, geography and geology of the coastline include both natural and man-made factors. Natural factors include river runoff wind, precipitation, surf, coastal vegetation, ice and changes in the World Ocean level. Man-made factors include construction of dams, mining, dredging, deforestation and engineering operations.

94 Coastal areas vary vastly. Some are flooded with water, such as deltas or mangroves, while some are relatively drier, like rocky shores. Yet, each area is affected by the unique interaction of land and marine elements. These are also areas of remarkable biodiversity. There are several unique plants, marine animals and coral reefs that can be seen in these areas.

95 The land–ocean interaction that we are most familiar with is **the beach.** A beach is a strip of land that gently slopes as it meets the edge of the ocean, river or lake. This is often a thriving ecosystem. Beaches were created on shorelines by deposits of sand, gravel, pebble stones or cobbles.

INTRODUCTION

96 Material on the beach is deposited over a long period of time and often comes from far off, carried by wind and waves. Tides bring in sediments such as shells, seaweed, sand and even organisms like crabs. This is a constant process where sediments are washed in and out of the beach strip.

97 The landscape of a beach—both above and below water—is known as the beach profile. It shows how a beach has been created over the years and how it has changed over the period of a single year! During winters, storm winds bring sediments and create sandbars. In summer, these sandbars are eroded and the beach is built again.

LAND INTERACTION: ROCKY SHORE, ICE EDGE, FJORD, MARSH, ESTUARY, WETLAND AND COASTAL FORESTS

98 **The beach profile is very interesting.** Farthest away from the shore, we have the foredune where water rarely reaches. Below this is a terrace called 'berms'. This is created by past storms. The lower terrace is the low tide terrace, part of which goes below the waterline. Then, there are submerged sandbars and troughs.

99 **A beach may seem like a simple sloping strip of land, but it is a lively ecosystem teeming with a variety of life forms.** We have seaweeds brought to the land by waves, vegetation on sand dunes and different birds and animals that nest on the beaches. Many animals and shellfish stay buried in the intertidal zone.

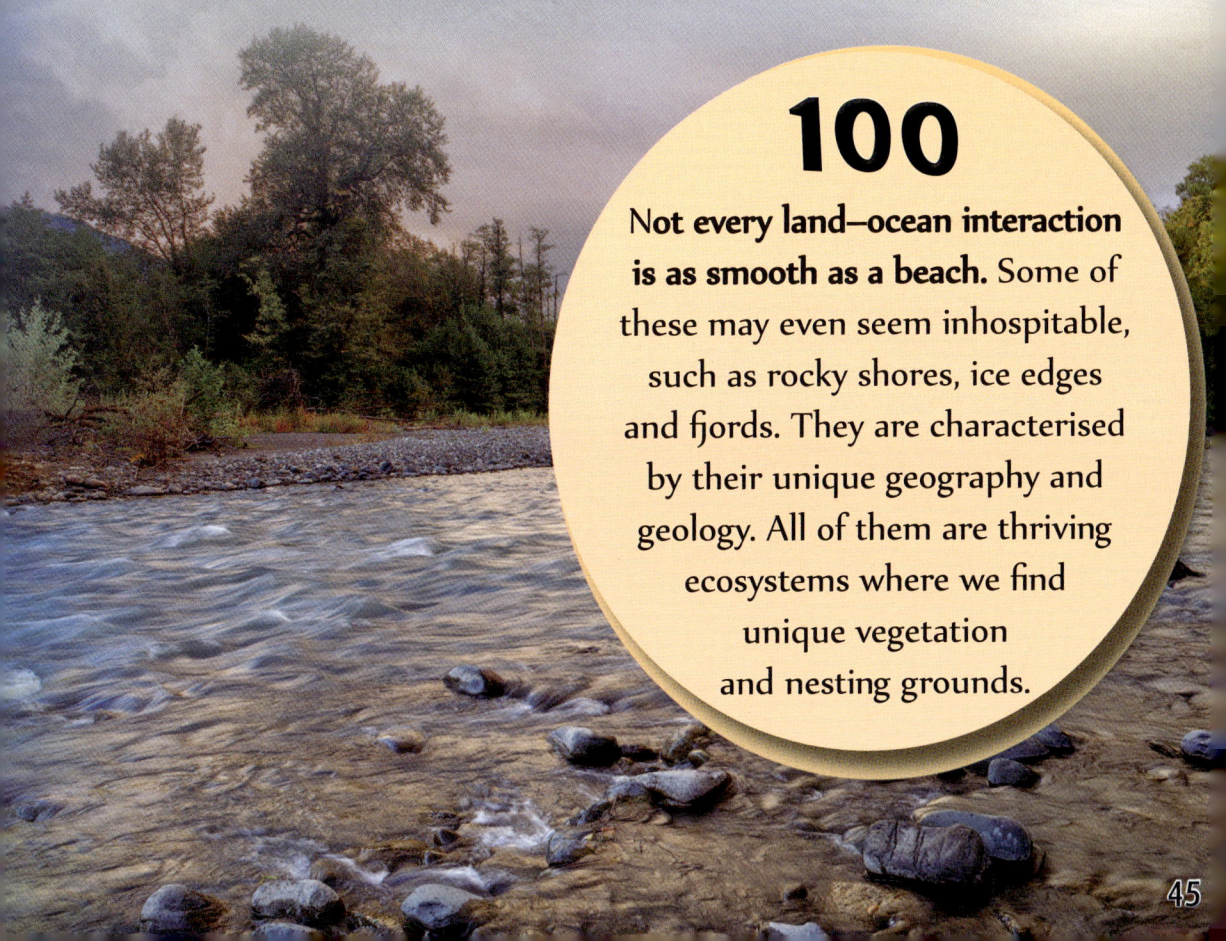

100 **Not every land–ocean interaction is as smooth as a beach.** Some of these may even seem inhospitable, such as rocky shores, ice edges and fjords. They are characterised by their unique geography and geology. All of them are thriving ecosystems where we find unique vegetation and nesting grounds.

INTRODUCTION

101 While we find sand on beaches, a rocky shore is characterised by solid rock on its intertidal areas. There are often boulders and rocky ledges. Life on the rocky shore is tough, but abundant. The area is exposed to the elements like harsh winds and strong waves.

102 Interestingly, we find that different zones on the beach support organisms with different adaptations. Those living near the high tide mark have adapted to high levels of air and sunlight exposure, but are not good at avoiding predators. Those at low tide mark are good at defence, but ill-suited for exposure to sunlight and air.

103 The diversity is quite limited above the intertidal zone. Here, you may find lichens or periwinkles. But life thrives at the intertidal zone, which gets a regular supply of nutrients through the waves. Here, we find invertebrates like barnacles, algae, birds and several mammals, which come here for shelter and nesting.

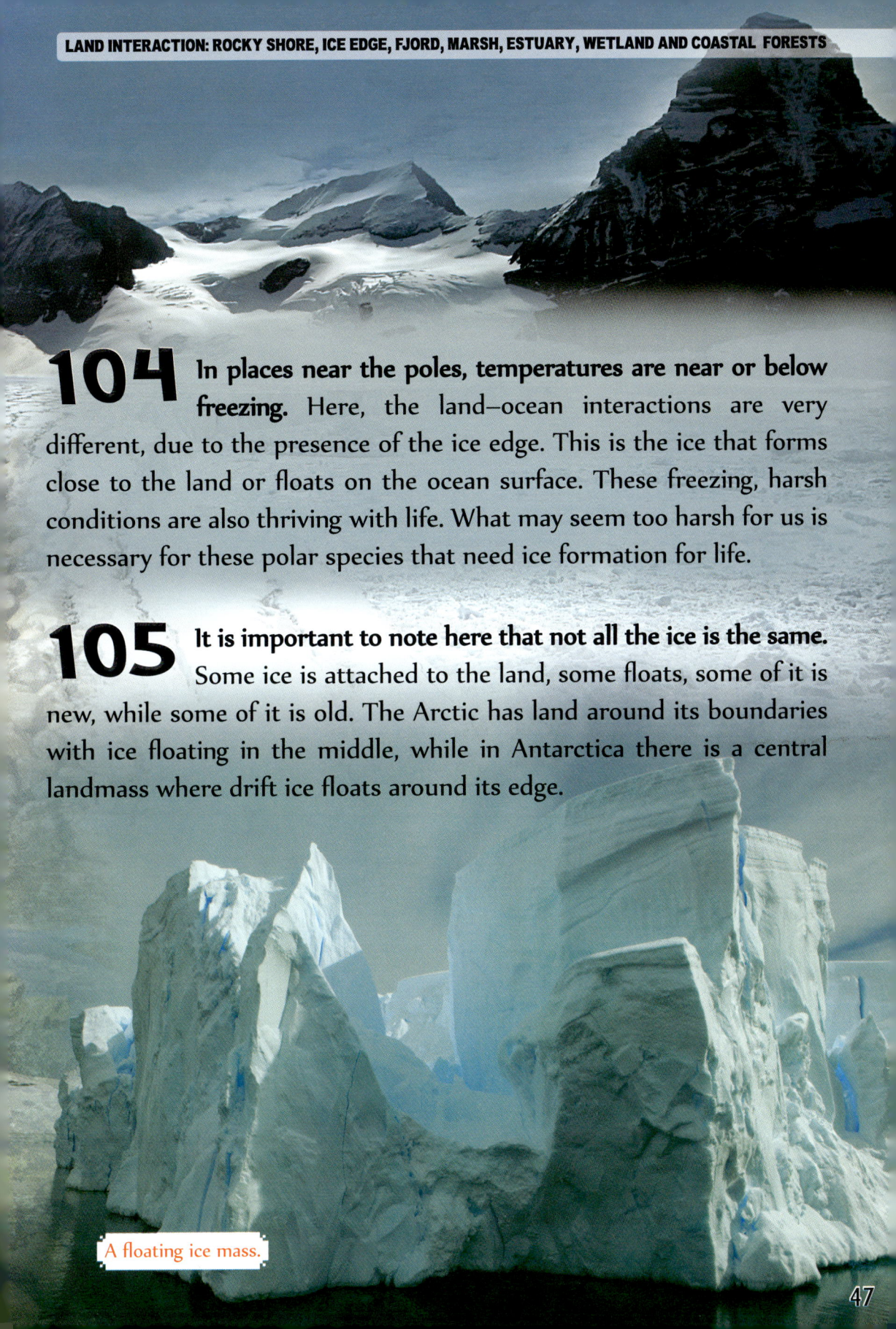

LAND INTERACTION: ROCKY SHORE, ICE EDGE, FJORD, MARSH, ESTUARY, WETLAND AND COASTAL FORESTS

104 **In places near the poles, temperatures are near or below freezing.** Here, the land–ocean interactions are very different, due to the presence of the ice edge. This is the ice that forms close to the land or floats on the ocean surface. These freezing, harsh conditions are also thriving with life. What may seem too harsh for us is necessary for these polar species that need ice formation for life.

105 **It is important to note here that not all the ice is the same.** Some ice is attached to the land, some floats, some of it is new, while some of it is old. The Arctic has land around its boundaries with ice floating in the middle, while in Antarctica there is a central landmass where drift ice floats around its edge.

A floating ice mass.

INTRODUCTION

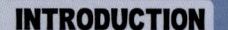

106 **These icy conditions are home to many unique animal and bird communities.** Mammals like penguins, seals, walruses and polar bears use it for shelter, rest and breeding. Planktons in the water underneath are an important food source for other species like krill and the blue whale. Interestingly, even moving ice creates life when it scares off habitats from the ocean floor, making space for new life.

107 A fjord is a long, deep inlet with steep cliffs on three sides. The opening towards the ocean is the mouth of the fjord, while the inner part is called the sea bottom. Its mouth is often shallow. A fjord is different from a bay or cove, because it has a narrow long formation.

LAND INTERACTION: ROCKY SHORE, ICE EDGE, FJORD, MARSH, ESTUARY, WETLAND AND COASTAL FORESTS

108 A fjord is formed when glaciers retreat from a valley. In the process, it creates a U-shaped valley which is then filled up by the sea. At its mouth, a fjord will usually have a sill caused by the glacier's erosion and deposits. This results in a shallow mouth and fjords that are often deeper than the adjacent sea.

109 Most fjords are found in the Northern Hemisphere because this is where most glaciers existed during the last ice age. The glaciers retreat and erosion created the fjords. They are most often found in Greenland, Canada and Northern Europe, most notably in Norway. In the southern hemisphere, we can find fjords in New Zealand and Chile.

110 The deep fjord basin allows deep sea creatures to live close to the shore, which is not possible near other coastlines. These include whales, sharks, seals, and several kinds of salmon. Recently, some deep water corals have also been found in fjords. These are old and slow growing corals that host a rich ecosystem of invertebrates and fishes.

49

INTRODUCTION

111 The edge of the ocean where it meets land is also the place where the ocean meets the rivers that drain into it. This creates unique ecosystems where the river and ocean environments meet each other. These places inundated with water are known as wetlands. Examples of wetlands are marshes, estuaries, mangroves, mudflats, deltas, lagoons, and floodplains.

112 Estuaries are partially enclosed bodies of brackish water where the rivers flow into the sea. The mix of marine water and freshwater results in the presence of nutrients and rich sediments. It creates a highly productive ecosystem. A number of animals use estuaries for food, breeding, and shelter. Incidentally, some of the most populated cities are also near estuaries.

LAND INTERACTION: ROCKY SHORE, ICE EDGE, FJORD, MARSH, ESTUARY, WETLAND AND COASTAL FORESTS

113
The fertility of estuary regions actually threatens the delicate balance of their ecosystems. Cities by estuaries are growing at a faster pace than those inland. This has created serious challenges, as population and pollution pressures can disturb the balance of its ecosystem, increasing the pressure on its precious natural resources.

114
Marshes are wetlands that are frequently or almost continuously flooded with water. They are characterised by plants that are adapted to saturated soil conditions with low oxygen levels. Marshes also support a variety of aquatic organisms, from invertebrates to fishes, mammals and amphibians. In fact, marshes support a fertile ecosystem.

115
Marshes are found near both seas and oceans. In both cases, they play a vital role in the environment. Apart from providing a habitat to a number of species, marshes are critical in acting as a buffer against heavy rainfall or storms, slowing erosion and absorbing excess nutrients and pollutants, so as to keep the chemical balance of the water intact.

INTRODUCTION

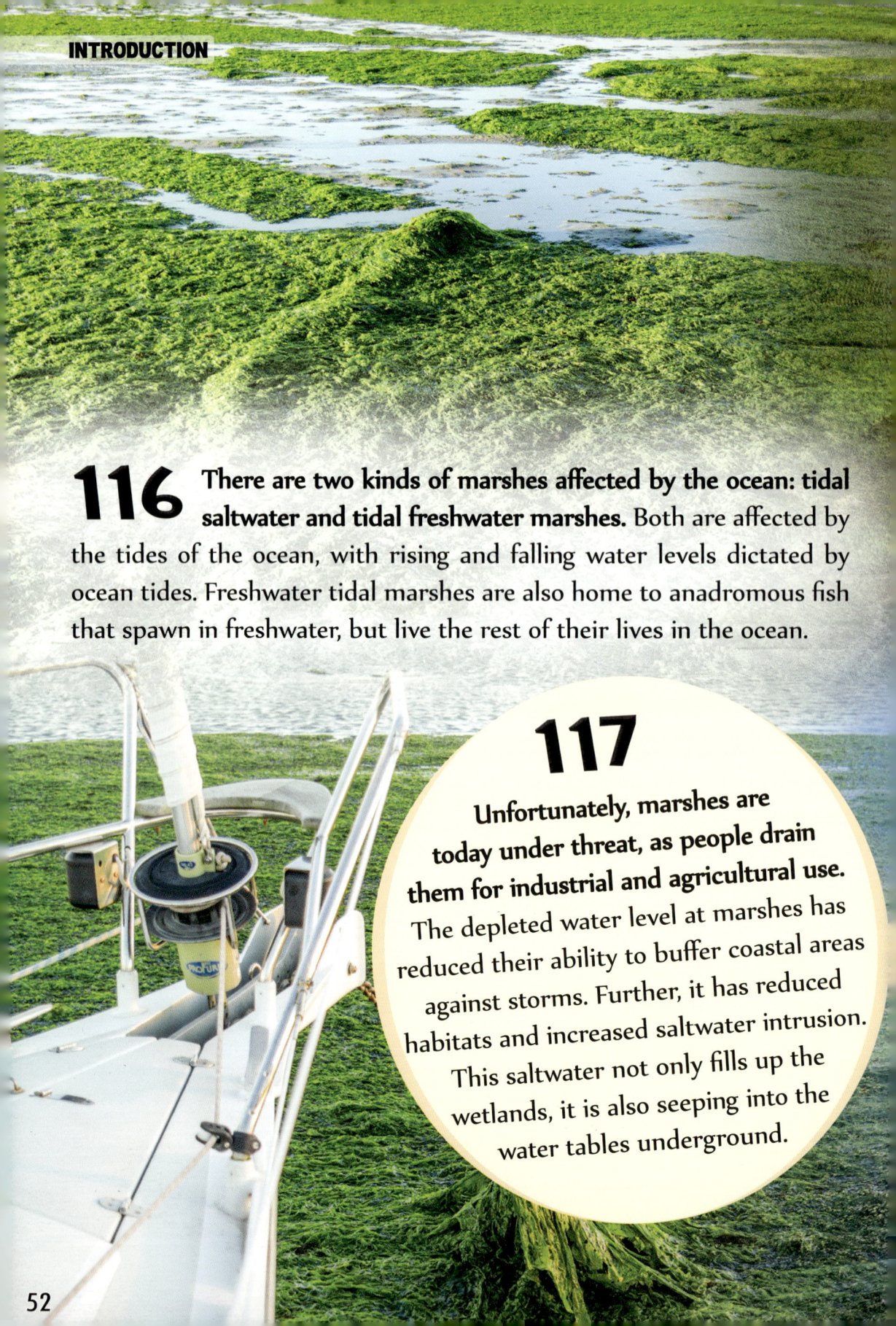

116 There are two kinds of marshes affected by the ocean: tidal saltwater and tidal freshwater marshes. Both are affected by the tides of the ocean, with rising and falling water levels dictated by ocean tides. Freshwater tidal marshes are also home to anadromous fish that spawn in freshwater, but live the rest of their lives in the ocean.

117 Unfortunately, marshes are today under threat, as people drain them for industrial and agricultural use. The depleted water level at marshes has reduced their ability to buffer coastal areas against storms. Further, it has reduced habitats and increased saltwater intrusion. This saltwater not only fills up the wetlands, it is also seeping into the water tables underground.

LAND INTERACTION: ROCKY SHORE, ICE EDGE, FJORD, MARSH, ESTUARY, WETLAND AND COASTAL FORESTS

118 **The places of confluence between a river and an ocean sometimes result in deltas.** Deltas are formed when a fast moving river meets standing or slow-moving water, like oceans, lakes or reservoirs. At this point, the accumulated sediment of the river is deposited and forms the delta. This is very fertile land.

119 **One of the most important and largest deltas in the world is the Ganges–Brahmaputra Delta.** Spanning Bangladesh and West Bengal in India, the delta has a number of rivers that drain into the Bay of Bengal, including the Ganges and the Brahmaputra. This is one of the world's most fertile regions and richest ecosystems.

120 **Oceans are vital to life on earth.** They may seem calm, but the waters of the oceans are always on the move, shaping our coastline and over a period of time, our continents. At the edge of the ocean, we have waterbodies like seas, bays or land interactions like wetlands. Thus, not just the vast oceans, but also the places where it meets the land, are important.

53

LIFE IN THE OCEANS

Plankton

121 Most of our planet is covered with oceans and is teeming with life. There are more than a million species living in our oceans and scientists say that we have not even explored most of these! Not just that, life in the ocean is colourful, unpredictable, strange and sometimes bizarre! Marine life is usually divided into two categories—plants and animals.

122 A glass of water from the ocean may seem clear, but actually, it has uncountable life forms inside it! For instance, it could be full of plankton. These are freshwater and marine organisms that are too small or weak to swim against the current. Most planktons are microscopic in size, but there are also some larger planktons like the jellyfish.

PLANKTON

123 **Planktons are a wide class of organisms that include both plants and animals.** These organisms are extremely vital for the freshwater and ocean ecosystem because they are an important food source for other marine life. Scientists are now exploring the uses of plankton in space travel!

124 **Planktons are broadly divided into four categories: phytoplankton, zooplankton, bacterioplankton and mycoplankton.** Phytoplankton are plant-like organisms, while zooplankton are animal-like organisms. Bacterioplankton include the bacteria and archaea, mycoplankton are fungus-like organisms.

125 **Phytoplankton are considered plant-like because they use photosynthesis to produce food.** This is why they are often found at or near the surface of the water. Marine phytoplankton include diatoms, dinoflagellates, cyanobacteria and coccolithophorids. It is estimated that phytoplankton contribute anywhere between 50–80 per cent of photosynthesis on earth! Hence, they are vital in maintaining the CO_2–O_2 balance on earth.

LIFE IN THE OCEANS

Zooplankton can be microscopic or as big as a jellyfish.

126 **Zooplankton are again divided into two groups: temporary zooplankton and permanent zooplankton.** Temporary zooplankton spend only a part of their life as planktons, such as eggs and larvae of certain organisms that float on the surface. Permanent planktons, on the other hand, spend their entire life as planktons. This is a wide class of organisms with millions of varieties existing.

127 **Bacterioplankton include bacteria and archaea, while mycoplankton are like fungi.** Together these planktons are vital in nutrient cycling. They convert dead organic material into plant nutrients. They recycle or extract other important nutrients in the water. This also makes them vital for the marine ecosystem, since the availability of nutrients makes the oceans capable of holding so much varied life.

Sample of a bacterioplankton.

Marine Mammals

128

The biggest mammals on earth are whales. Like all mammals, they are warm blooded, have mammary glands and hair (although very little). They are also extremely intelligent. They have blowholes on top of their head through which they breathe in air. Although whales seem to have evolved from land animals, they are completely adapted to marine life and incapable of surviving on land.

129

The Blue Whale is the largest mammal on earth. They can grow 100 feet long and weigh more than 200 tonnes. They may swim in small pods, pairs or alone. They are also one of the noisiest creatures on the planet, often groaning, moaning, crying or calling out to each other! They also live a long life, close to 80–90 years.

130

The Beluga Whale is distinctive for its white colour and prominent forehead. It is one of the smallest species among whales. They are social animals that live in small pods. They also have a uniquely flexible neck that allows them to turn their head in all directions. The beluga whales are found in the Arctic Ocean.

LIFE IN THE OCEANS

131 Known for its massive head, the Bowhead Whale is found in the chilly whalers of the Arctic Ocean. So massive is its skull that it can amount to a third of its total body weight! It uses its skull to break through the ice on the ocean surface. It grows up to 50 feet and weighs up to 80 tonnes.

132 Despite its name the Killer Whale is not actually a whale! In fact, it is a large dolphin. However, unlike most friendly dolphins we know, the killer whale is an aggressive and fearsome predator. It is also a very intelligent mammal that exhibits a complex social structure. They are one of the most widespread animal species, found in all oceans.

133 With its long tusk, the Narwhal stands out among sea animals. The tusk is actually found only in males. It is a modification of two upper teeth, that can reach up to six feet! They are found in the Arctic Ocean where they hunt close to the edge of the ice bank. Narwhals are facing extinction due to climate changes.

MARINE MAMMALS

134 One of the most recognised and loved marine animal is the Bottlenose Dolphin. The coastal dolphins live in all kinds of ecosystems, from seagrass beds to estuaries. Oceanic dolphins are more migratory in nature. The bottlenose dolphin is extremely intelligent and curious. It lives in a highly complex social system.

135 Dugong is a kind of sea cow that is found in the warm waters of the Indian and Western Pacific Ocean. This herbivorous sea animal is found on the ocean bed, feeding on seagrass. Reaching 13 feet in length and more than one metric ton in weight, the adult dugong has almost no natural predators.

136 The Hourglass Dolphin gets its name from the distinctive white and black markings on its body that resemble an hourglass. It lives in one of the coldest places on earth—the Antarctic Ocean. This is a very rarely seen species. In fact, the only evidence scientists have that it exists at all is through other witnesses!

LIFE IN THE OCEANS

137 The Pantropical Spotted Dolphin is found throughout tropical oceans of the world. The species has a wide range in size and colour. Like most dolphin species, they are also extremely social, living in large pods and often travelling with tuna fish. Once endangered, the pantropical spotted dolphin has today been declared out of danger.

138 The Grey Whale actually looks like a weathered ocean rock. It gets this colour not just because of its skin, but also due to the tiny organisms and parasites that cover its body. The grey whale is also known for its long migration paths. They are known to travel over 12,430 miles on their annual migratory journeys.

139 Found in the temperate regions of the Indian, Atlantic and Pacific Oceans, the Risso's Dolphin lives at the depth of 1,500–3,300 feet. The pups are grey-brown, but by the time they grow up they appear almost completely white. This is because of the scarring on their body due to social interactions.

MARINE MAMMALS

140 **Found in the frigidly cold environment of the Antarctic Ocean, the Southern Elephant Seal is the largest seal in the world.** The adult male is more than 20 feet long and can weigh up to 8,800 pounds. The male seal is very territorial and lives with a harem of females. They also often engage in aggressive fights for dominance.

141 **Found in every ocean, from the Arctic to the Antarctic, the Humpback Whale has quite a worldwide distribution.** At 50 feet, it is also among the largest animals weighs 80 tonnes in the world. But the humpback whale is unique in many ways, especially for its singing! The songs of humpback whales are intricate, complex and carry over large distances.

142 **The second largest animal to ever live on earth is the Fin Whale.** Despite its enormous size at 45 feet and weight of 80 tonnes it is quite a fast swimmer. It is found in almost all oceans, except the Arctic. Fin whales also live quite a long life, almost 150 years! They are known for their unique colouration and sleek body.

LIFE IN THE OCEANS

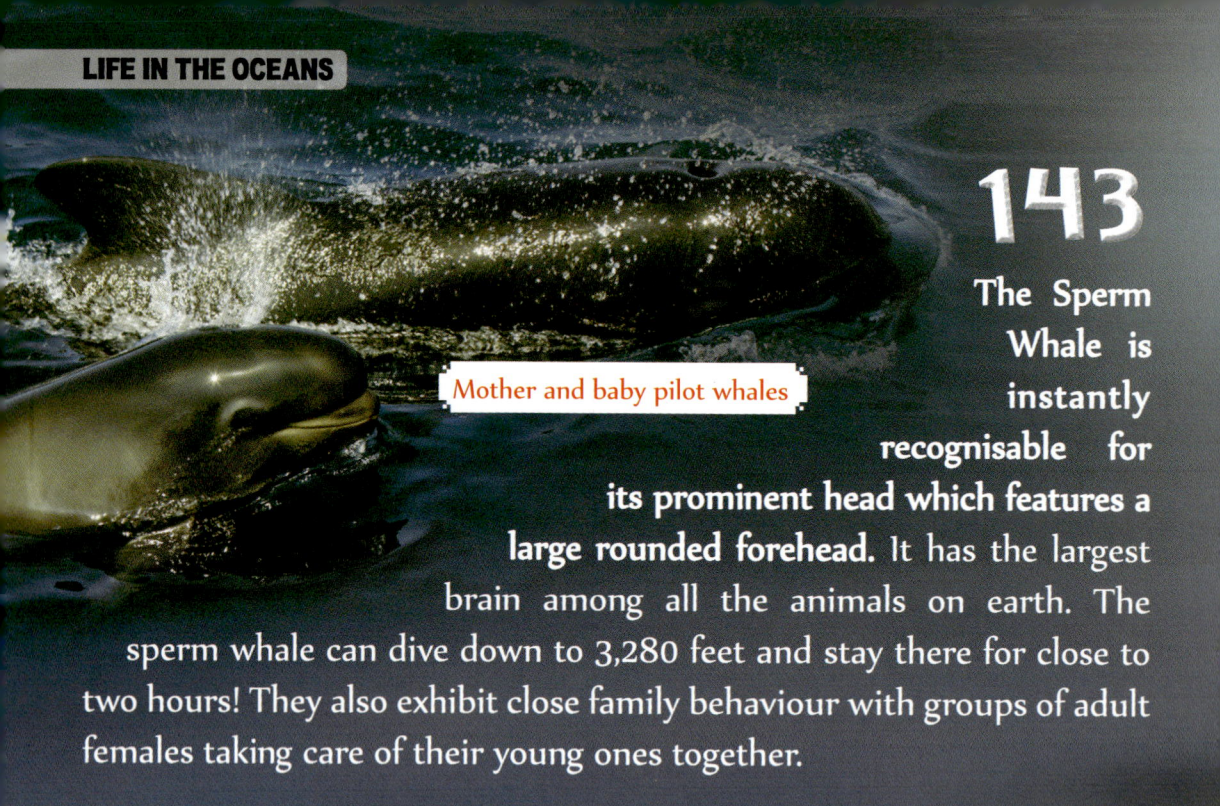

Mother and baby pilot whales

143 **The Sperm Whale is instantly recognisable for its prominent head which features a large rounded forehead.** It has the largest brain among all the animals on earth. The sperm whale can dive down to 3,280 feet and stay there for close to two hours! They also exhibit close family behaviour with groups of adult females taking care of their young ones together.

144 **Despite its name, a Pilot Whale is actually a dolphin.** In fact, they are among the largest species of dolphins. They get their name from their habit of following a 'pilot' or leader. These social creatures live in pods of up to 100 members and also socialise with other whale species. They are known for their intelligence.

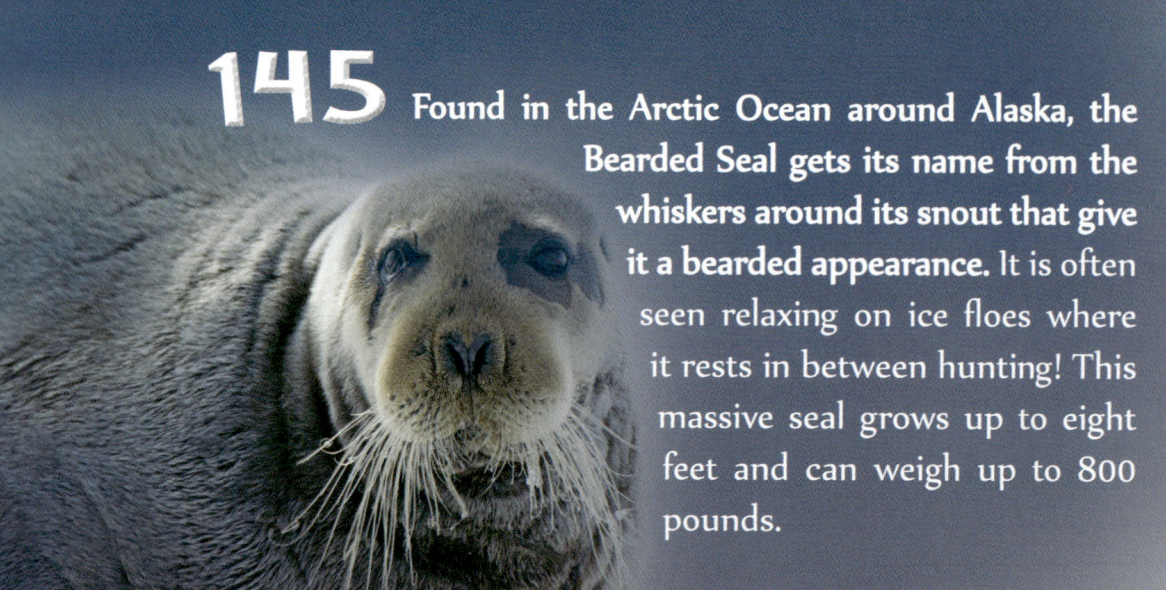

145 **Found in the Arctic Ocean around Alaska, the Bearded Seal gets its name from the whiskers around its snout that give it a bearded appearance.** It is often seen relaxing on ice floes where it rests in between hunting! This massive seal grows up to eight feet and can weigh up to 800 pounds.

MARINE MAMMALS

146 Found on the shores of the North Atlantic Ocean, the Grey Seals are not actually named for their colour. Their name is actually Latin for 'hook-nosed sea pig'. As true seals, they do not have external ear flaps and move by dragging themselves on their belly. Despite their massive size, they are agile divers and hunters.

147 Found in the Arctic and Atlantic Oceans, the Harp Seal gets its name from the harp-shaped markings on its back. Adult seals have a dark-coloured pelt, while the pups are white. The females gather in large colonies to give birth to their young ones. They are highly migratory, undertaking journeys of 4,000 kilometres every year!

LIFE IN THE OCEANS

148 Unlike most seal species, the Hawaiian Monk Seals prefer the warmer Hawaiian Islands to frigid cold weather conditions. Found in the remote and uninhabited northwestern Hawaiian Islands, they are also unique in their preference for a more solitary life. They are critically endangered with a close cousin, the Caribbean Monk seal, which is already extinct.

149 As is obvious, the Leopard Seal gets its name from the spots on its skin. It also shares the aggressive fighting instincts of its namesake. Found in the Antarctic, it is the top predator of the region. It is an excellent swimmer and often hunts large-sized prey. At 10–11.5 feet, they have a fairly long body with a prominent head.

150 The Sea Otter is the only member of the weasel family that spends almost all of its life in the ocean. These adorable looking creatures have a number of oddities. Otters are often found in a group, floating on their back in kelp forests, to keep afloat. When eating, the otters place a rock on their stomach to smash shellfish and eat them!

MARINE MAMMALS

151 Also known as sea cows, the Manatees are herbivorous and languid, just like their land namesakes. Manatees are 13.1 feet in length and weighs up to 590 kilograms. Despite their bulk the manatee is a quick and agile swimmer. Manatees almost never leave water. They even give birth underwater. But, like all sea animals, they need to come to the surface frequently to breathe.

A young manatee

152 With its moustache and long tusk, the Walrus is quite distinctive. Its tusks are actually elongated canine teeth. The tusks are not just for show, however. They have multiple uses, from fighting and digging holes in ice, to climbing over ice floes. Their whiskers are also useful. They are used to detect prey in the dark ocean floor.

153 At 10 feet in length and 1,000 kilograms in weight, the Steller Sea Lion is the largest sea lion species. These creatures are voracious eaters. They are social animals and live in groups. Dominant males keep harem of females for breeding. When stellar sea lions come ashore for breeding, they make a lot of noise and show aggression, in order to establish dominance.

LIFE IN THE OCEANS

154 The smallest of the sea lions, the Galápagos Sea Lions, are found almost exclusively on the Galápagos Islands. They are known for their playful and social nature, often heard barking and playing in water. The Galápagos sea lions are of two types—territorial and non-territorial. Their bark is used to establish dominance and territory.

155 A smaller cousin of the whale and dolphin, the Vaquita is usually four-five feet long, weighing not more than 45 kilograms. The vaquita are found in the north of the Gulf of California, Mexico. The vaquitas are now listed as critically endangered because of their falling numbers.

Corals and Other Invertebrates

156 **The ocean is colourful and full of life.** In fact, life exists in unexpected places underwater. Even the stones that look inanimate are actually full of life, giving colour and character to our ocean floor. Some of the colourful and fascinating life forms are the corals and other invertebrates like jellyfish, starfish, sea slugs, kelp and more.

157 **Have you seen pictures of beautiful, coloured stones on the ocean floor?** Chances are that those were not stones, but animals! Corals are animals that stay in one place throughout their life. The body of a coral is called a polyp. On its top are tentacles. Some corals live alone, while some live in large colonies. Many colonies together form a coral reef.

158 **Found in the deep sea near fjords, the Cockscomb Cup Coral builds reefs, which attract fish and invertebrates.** When present with other corals in a reef, they are often the most common variety. They feed on plankton that flows throw the reef. This stony coral has a skeleton of calcium carbonate, which makes it susceptible to increasing acidification of our oceans.

LIFE IN THE OCEANS

159 Like its name suggests, the Grooved Brain Coral looks remarkably like the human brain. The grooves and twists on its surface, coupled with its dome-like shape, give it the appearance of a brain sitting on the ocean floor. The major difference is that they can be as big as six feet! This coral is actually a colony of several identical animals living together.

160 The Ivory Bush Coral is found in both shallow and deep ocean water. Hence, they utilise different means of feeding. In shallow water they depend on algae for food, while in deep water they feed on floating plankton. The Ivory Bush Coral forms an important habitat for many fish and invertebrates, many of which are commercially important.

Lobe Coral

161 The Lobe Coral is known for its size. Found in the tropical waters of the Indo-Pacific Ocean, this species forms massive structures or colonies. However, only a few millimetres of the outer layer of this coral are actually living. Most of it is composed of the calcium carbonate skeleton. These creatures feed through symbiotic algae as well as on zooplanktons.

CORALS AND OTHER INVERTEBRATES

162 **Found on the deep ocean floor, the Lophelia Coral builds enormous reefs.** Some of these reefs are several miles long and as high as 100 feet. The coral grows very slowly and lives for years, sometimes as long as 1,000 years! There are massive colonies in our oceans that might be even older! Like most deep water corals, they also feed on planktons.

Staghorn Coral

163 **One of the fastest growing corals in the world is the Staghorn Coral.** The colonies look like stag horns and together they form enormous reefs. They grow quite fast and are often the most impressive in shallow tropical waters where they are found. On the flip side, the reef structures are quite delicate and susceptible to damage.

164 **Found in almost all the oceans, the Sea Pen is a soft coral.** It includes several species and shows remarkable polymorphism. In larger colonies a polyp grows and then loses its tentacles. It then becomes the central axis of the colony with several other polyps of different shapes and functions growing on it.

69

LIFE IN THE OCEANS

165 The Starfish is not actually a fish. In fact, it is closer to sand dollars and sea urchins. Hence, scientists now call it the Sea Star. Unlike fish, sea stars are also invertebrates. They have a hard, bony skin. Together with their bright colours, it forms a deterrent against predators.

166 Did you know, the vital organs of a Sea Star are stored in its limbs! This allows the creature to regenerate its entire body from any severed limb! Although it is the five-armed sea star that is more familiar, there are stars with as many as 50 arms! The arms have suckers and pincers that help in movement.

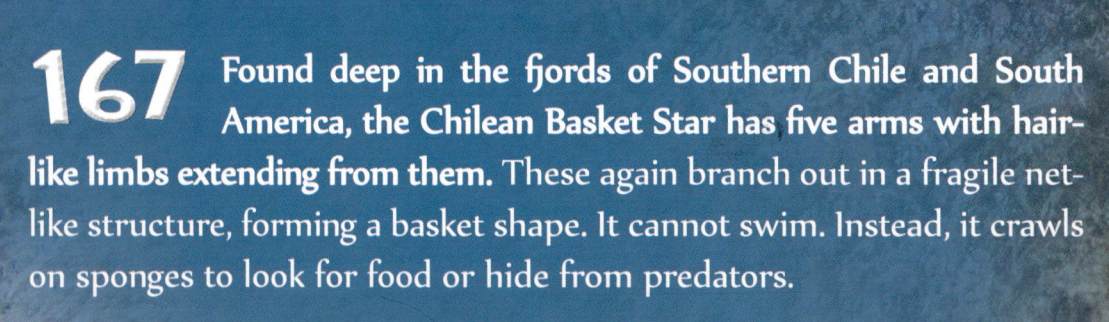

167 Found deep in the fjords of Southern Chile and South America, the Chilean Basket Star has five arms with hair-like limbs extending from them. These again branch out in a fragile net-like structure, forming a basket shape. It cannot swim. Instead, it crawls on sponges to look for food or hide from predators.

CORALS AND OTHER INVERTEBATES

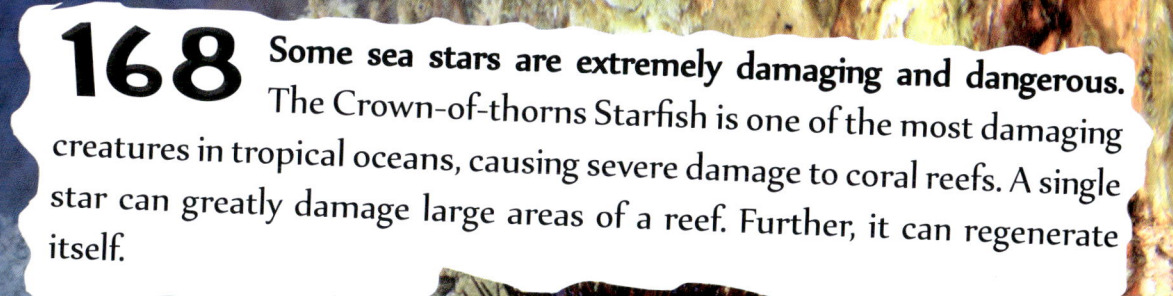

168 **Some sea stars are extremely damaging and dangerous.** The Crown-of-thorns Starfish is one of the most damaging creatures in tropical oceans, causing severe damage to coral reefs. A single star can greatly damage large areas of a reef. Further, it can regenerate itself.

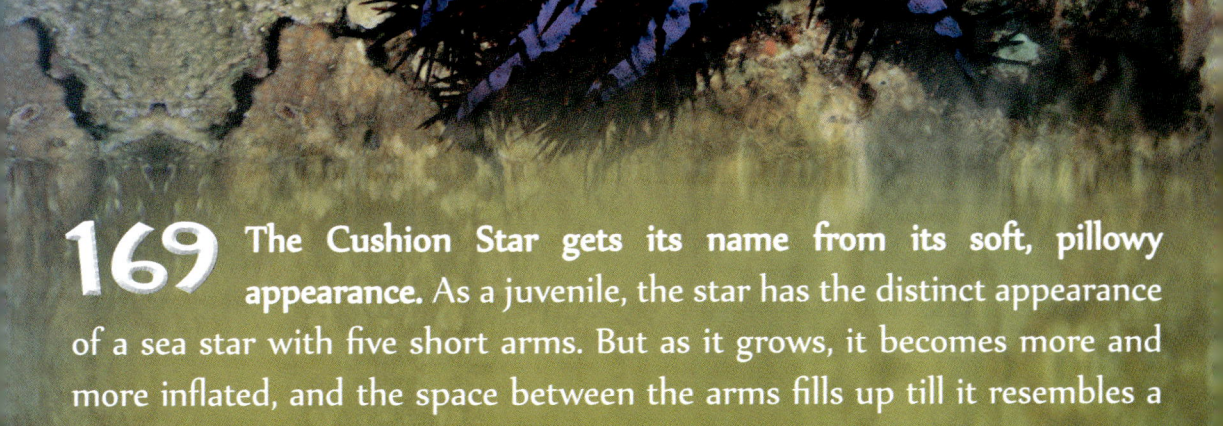

169 **The Cushion Star gets its name from its soft, pillowy appearance.** As a juvenile, the star has the distinct appearance of a sea star with five short arms. But as it grows, it becomes more and more inflated, and the space between the arms fills up till it resembles a pentagonal pincushion.

LIFE IN THE OCEANS

170

The Sea Anemone is striking with its brilliant flashy colours. But appearances are deceptive. Its cylindrical body is topped by stinging tentacles that surround its mouth. The tentacles are used to sting its prey with neurotoxins and then guide it to its mouth. There are more than 1,000 sea anemone species found in all colours and sizes.

171
Found in the Caribbean Sea, the giant Caribbean Sea Anemone is found either on the ocean floor or in coral reefs. Although it is a predatory creature, it does have a symbiotic relationship with sea creatures like cleaner shrimps and juvenile cardinal fish. When under attack, it can close its tentacles to form a ball.

172
Found in the Indo-Pacific Ocean, the Giant Carpet Anemone thrives on seagrass beds and coral reefs. This species is known for its symbiotic relationship with many sea creatures. For example, the green algae living on it provide it with energy, while the anemone provides the algae with nutrients. It is also home to many symbiotic anemone fish.

CORALS AND OTHER INVERTEBATES

173 Did you know that you can find Sponges in the ocean? A sponge is one of the oldest living animals on earth! These are simple creatures with no digestive, nervous or circulatory system. They have pores and channels that allow them to filter water for nutrition and push out waste. There are over 5,000 species of sea sponges found worldwide.

174 At over three feet, the Yellow Tube Sponge is counted among the larger sponge species. It gets its name from its appearance, as it has a yellowish body. At depths one can also find it in a brilliant yellowish blue colour. It has a tube-like structure. Like other sponges, they stay attached to a reef throughout their life.

LIFE IN THE OCEANS

175 As the name suggest, the Giant Barrel Sponge is literally gigantic reaching over six feet in size! Found on coral reefs around the Caribbean Sea, it has a bowl-like structure, which is open at the top. It often forms the habitat for a number of other invertebrates and fish. It has a long life—more than a thousand years!

176 Popular for its delicate, lattice-like structure, the Venus' Flower Basket gets its name from this very structure. Its skeleton is made of silica and covered by a thin cellular layer. The skeleton of the venus' flower basket is a prized commodity for its delicacy, especially in Japanese culture where it is seen as a symbol of eternal love.

CORALS AND OTHER INVERTEBATES

177 Found worldwide, the Red Boring Sponge can appear on rocky ocean bottoms as well as on the shells of corals and molluscs. When the larvae of this sponge settle on the coral or mollusc, they burrow or 'bore' in by secreting sulphuric acid. Thus, they eat away at the shell, disintegrating the host and spreading out on its remains.

178 The biggest family of invertebrates in the ocean are Molluscs. This is a very wide class of creatures and they come in all shapes, sizes, habitats and behaviours. Molluscs are creatures with skeletons or exoskeletons. The biggest invertebrate, the giant squid, is a mollusc. Some molluscs like snails are also found on land.

179 Considered a delicacy by some, Oysters are invertebrate creatures found all over the world. Usually oysters are oval, but some take the shape of whatever they are attached to. Oysters have very strong adductor muscles, which help them in closing their shells when under threat.

LIFE IN THE OCEANS

180 Though they are usually abundant in eastern North American coastal waters, the population of American oysters has recently been severely depleted. Like other varieties of oysters, it has a short mobile phase when juvenile. Then it settles on a hard surface, often as dead oyster shells. Through this process, it forms large reefs which in turn form the habitat for other sea creatures.

American Oysters

181 Although the Pearl Oysters look like edible oysters, they are not closely related at all. Do you know how an oyster creates a pearl? When an intruder, like a sand grain, enters the shell, the oyster quickly covers it with a layer called nacre to avoid irritation. Over time, layers of nacre cover the grain, forming an iridescent pearl!

Pearl Oysters

CORALS AND OTHER INVERTERBATES

182 Similar to the oyster, but different in many essential aspects is another mollusc, the Clam. This is a highly varied family with several different species. Like oysters, clams have two equal-sized shells connected by adductor muscles. Most clams spend their life partially buried in the ocean floor. They come in different shapes and have different lifespans. They can live from a year to centuries!

183 With a size measuring over four-and-a-half feet, and roughly 250 kilograms in weight, the Giant Clam lives up to its name. Apart from its size, the brilliant colours of the clam also make it noticeable. Found on coral reefs, it has a symbiotic relationship with algae that live in its cells.

Sea Urchin

184 Sea Urchins are found across all oceans, except the colder regions. They are found on rocky ocean floor and corals. There are roughly 200 sea urchin species known to us. Some have a spiky outer layer, while others have plates. They are omnivorous, eating both plants and animals. Interestingly, they do not have a brain. Instead, they rely on a water vascular system for their life systems.

LIFE IN THE OCEANS

185 Did you know that the invertebrates that are closest to vertebrates like us are sea urchins named Sand Dollars? Yes, these small disk-like creatures are among our closest cousins! Instead of long spines, their body is covered with short fuzzy hair, which acts like spines. They are usually found crowded together and burrowing in the ocean floor.

Sand dollars breathe through their spine.

186 Sea Cucumbers are not actually marine vegetables! These marine animals get their name from their tubular structure. They play an important role in the marine ecosystem, breaking down waste material and other organic matter. When under threat, sea cucumbers can take extreme action, often mutilating their own bodies! They also eject a sticky substance to trap their enemy.

187 Nudibranchs are some of the most alien looking creatures on this planet. There are more than 3,000 species around the world and each is more wildly colourful than the other! These jelly-bodied molluscs get their wonderful colours from the food they eat. Some of them even retain the toxins of their prey and eject it when under threat!

CORALS AND OTHER INVERTERBATES

188 The floating, luminescent Jellyfish is a really old creature, older than the dinosaurs! It has an umbrella-shaped upper body with tentacles that trail below. The tentacles have tiny stinging cells that are used to stun the prey. Jellyfishes have an incredibly fast digestive system to ensure that their bodies remain light enough to float.

A jellyfish

189 One of the most brilliant and mysterious creatures of the ocean are the Pyrosomes. This tubular, glowing white creature is actually a colony of hundreds of clones known as zooids. They are joined together in a gelatinous tunic, moving and working as one. They are also bioluminescent. One luminescent body can trigger all its neighbours to light up!

190 Reaching heights of over 100 feet, the Giant Kelp forms green forests at the ocean floor, which serves as a habitat for many creatures. This marine algae looks very much like grass. Like grass, it gets its energy from photosynthesis. Capable of growing really fast, it forms an important marine habitat and source of food.

Celaphods, Crustaceans and Other Shellfish

191 Found in tidal or shallow waters, Barnacles are often mistaken as molluscs because of their hard shell. But they are closer to crabs, krills and lobsters! They have some mobility when they are juvenile, but later attach themselves to whatever substrate they are on—from whales and crabs, to rocks. Some species are parasitic, but most are harmless filter feeders.

192 One of the most familiar creatures of the sea are Crabs. There are more than 6,700 species of crabs and these are divided into 93 different groups. They are usually found in coral reefs and rocky pools. Apart from a thick shell on its body, a crab also has armoured claws at the front, which it uses to catch its prey.

CELAPHODS, CRUSTACEANS AND OTHER SHELLFISH

193 King Crabs are known for their huge size. In fact, only a few species are actually that big. For instance, the blue king crab can weigh up to eight kilograms! They are usually found in the warmer oceans of the southern hemisphere, apart from the Alaskan king crab. There are more than 40 species of king crab and these are considered a delicacy.

194 Most Hermit Crabs live in the ocean—from the deep sea bottom to coastal waters—but a few also live on land. This creature has a soft, spiral abdomen. It uses a borrowed or abandoned shell on its back to protect its soft abdomen and keep its gills moist. It even fights with other crabs for the shell!

195 At 16–20 kilograms, the Japanese Giant Spider Crab is the largest crab in the world. It has got its name from the fact that its eight legs make it look like a spider. At 13 feet from tip to tip, it is truly a giant. It is called a giant because of its long legs too.

LIFE IN THE OCEANS

The Caribbean Spiny Lobster

196 Closely related to shrimps and crabs, Lobsters are 10-legged crustaceans. These bottom-dwelling creatures are not just found in all the oceans, but also in freshwater. Lobsters have terrible eyesight, but they compensate for this with an excellent sense of smell and taste. Lobster larvae live in burrows or hide in seagrass, where they spend the rest of their lives.

197 The Caribbean Spiny Lobster is found in seagrass beds and coral reefs. The shell of the lobster is actually a skeleton that is formed outside the body. Since it cannot expand, the lobster must shed the skeleton regularly as it grows. The new skeleton grows from within the old one and as it becomes too big, it cracks open the old shell.

CELAPHODS, CRUSTACEANS AND OTHER SHELLFISH

198 At 46 feet and 500 kilograms, the Colossal Squid is just slightly smaller than the giant squid. However, it does share the record of the largest eyes in the animal kingdom with its giant cousin. Their huge eyes allow the squids to see in the murky depths of the ocean. The colossal squid have been found in the depths of the Antarctic Ocean.

199 After the giant and colossal squids, comes the Jumbo Squid or, as it is better known, the Humboldt Squid. It is seven feet long and can weigh up to 50 kilograms. Like all squids, they grow really fast. Humboldt squid can also change its colour from red to purple to white. Some scientists believe that this is a communication method!

200 One of the most mysterious creatures of the deep ocean is the Giant Squid. The largest squid of this kind to be discovered was 59 feet in length and nearly 900 kilograms in weight, making it the largest invertebrate. We know very little about them because they live in the very depths of the ocean. However, their carcasses have been found in all oceans.

Giant Squid

LIFE IN THE OCEANS

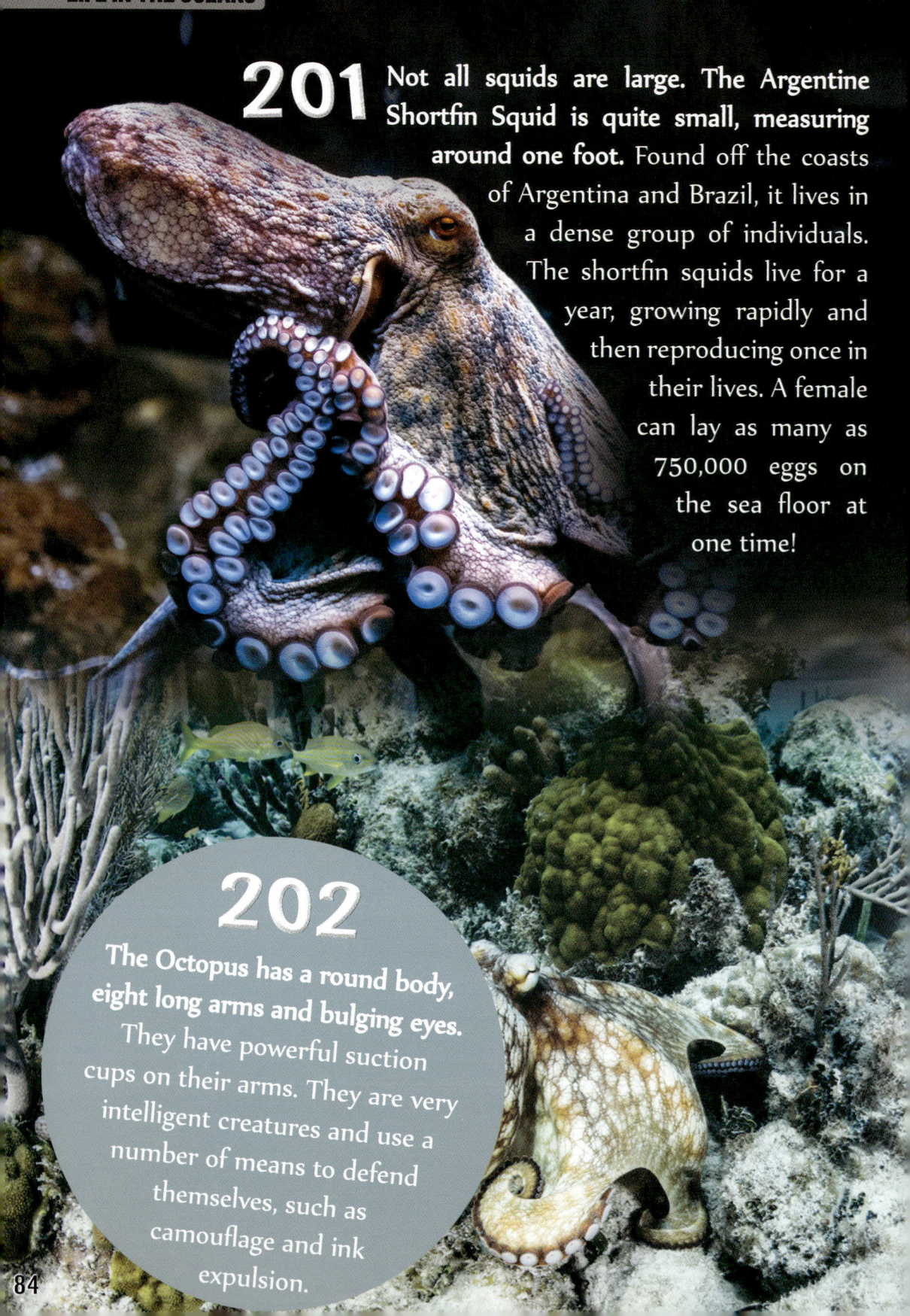

201
Not all squids are large. The Argentine Shortfin Squid is quite small, measuring around one foot. Found off the coasts of Argentina and Brazil, it lives in a dense group of individuals. The shortfin squids live for a year, growing rapidly and then reproducing once in their lives. A female can lay as many as 750,000 eggs on the sea floor at one time!

202
The Octopus has a round body, eight long arms and bulging eyes. They have powerful suction cups on their arms. They are very intelligent creatures and use a number of means to defend themselves, such as camouflage and ink expulsion.

CELAPHODS, CRUSTACEANS AND OTHER SHELLFISH

203 **There are few species as adept at camouflage as the Caribbean Reef Octopus.** Not only can it change colours to match its surroundings, it can also work its skin and muscle to create the same texture! This predatory species can also become cannibalistic, especially when its territory is threatened.

204 **There are over 2,000 species of Shrimp, some are so small that we cannot see them! They are found at the bottom of the oceans and riverbeds.** They have a hard, transparent shell which makes them nearly invisible in water. They live in large groups of individuals, called a school. Shrimp are omnivorous, mainly feeding on algae, planktons and tiny fishes.

Chambered Nautilus

205 Unlike most shelled invertebrates, the Chambered Nautilus lives in water columns of the open oceans and not on the reef surface or seafloor. When under threat, the nautilus retracts into its shell. Interestingly, it lives only in the outer chamber of the shell. The rest of the chambers are filled with air to keep it floating!

LIFE IN THE OCEANS

206 Found on the shores of the Western Europe the common Limpet is actually a marine snail. It has a strong, muscular foot that forms such strong attachment to the rocks of its habitat that predators find it difficult to pick up. Its conical shell offers another layer of protection. The shell is hard and difficult to grip.

207 Some marine snails are eye-catching and colourful, such as the Flamingo Tongue. It is found on coral reefs in the Atlantic Ocean. The flamingo tongue is named so because of its colours: pink or orange with black spots. The colours come from the soft tissue that covers its shell.

CELAPHODS, CRUSTACEANS AND OTHER SHELLFISH

208 At one-and-a-half feet in length, the Giant Triton is one of the largest marine snails. It is an aggressive hunter, detecting its prey through its excellent sense of smell. It is the only natural predator of the reef-destroying crown-of-thorn starfish. Hence, it is considered important in preventing outbreaks of crown-of-thorn starfish.

209 Found in the Indo-West Pacific Ocean, the Tiger Prawn is an invasive species highly valued as seafood. The female lays thousands of eggs, which hatch quickly. Like lobsters, the shell covering the the body of a tiger prawn is a skeleton, which it sheds regularly as it grows in size. This is a omnivorous creature and eats a variety of food.

210 Did you know that the combined weight of the Antarctic Krill is more than that of humans on earth? The krill is vital to the marine ecosystem because of its role in the food chain. It is placed near the bottom of the marine food chain, as it feeds on phytoplankton, and is the main food source of a number of ocean creatures.

Ocean Fishes

211 Found in the Atlantic and Pacific Oceans, Salmon is prized as seafood. Yet, it is actually born in freshwater, after which it migrates to the sea. It returns to freshwater to breed. In the process, some salmon species travel 7,000 feet upstream. Some subspecies stay on in freshwater. Salmon feeds on insects, invertebrates, shrimps and other fish.

212 The Sockeye Salmon is among the smaller salmon species. Like other salmons, they are born in freshwater. But unlike other salmons, juvenile sockeyes stay on in freshwater for three years. Sea-going sockeyes are silver-coloured, but as they swim upriver, they turn bright red with a greenish head.

Sockeye salmon on its way to the spawning ground.

213 The Chinook Salmon is the largest among the salmons found in the Pacific region with a length of 4.5 feet and weighing 55 kilograms. During its life in the ocean, the chinook salmon focuses on feeding and storing energy. At maturity, it can swim thousands of mile upstream to their breeding areas. So difficult is the journey that the salmons die immediately after laying their eggs.

OCEAN FISHES

214 Did you know that it is the male Seahorse that gives birth? The male seahorse has a brood pouch in which the female deposits its eggs. The male releases the juvenile seahorse after the egg hatches! Clearly, the seahorse's body shape is not its only unusual feature. Did you know, unlike most other fish, it also mates for life!

The unusual and unique seahorse.

215 Living in the deep sea, the Oarfish is rarely seen. In fact, the only time we have seen it is when it gets washed up on shores, dead or nearly dead. It is the longest bony fish, with some individuals reported as long as 50 feet and 272 kilograms in weight. It has a long, narrow body with silver-coloured scales and red fins.

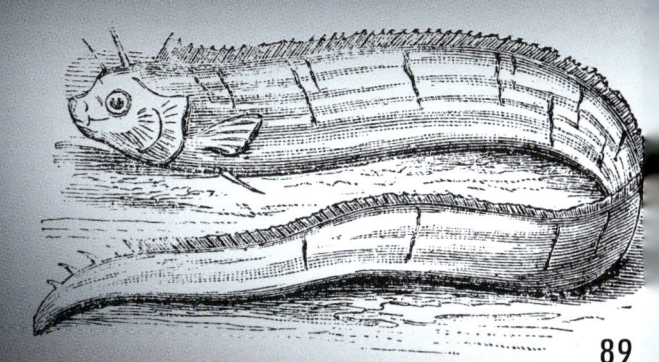

LIFE IN THE OCEANS

216 The Red Snapper is an aggressive predator and eats almost every fish smaller than it. They are voracious feeders with large mouths and sharp teeth. Most red snappers travel in dense schools. The most well known variety of red snapper is the northern red snapper. Found in the Gulf of Mexico, it reaches over three feet in size.

217 At eight feet in length and 320 kilograms in weight, it is easy to see how the Atlantic Goliath Grouper got its name. It lives along mangrove forests and coral reefs of the Atlantic Ocean, where it is one of the largest predators. It has a large mouth, which it uses to create pressure, sucking in its prey and swallowing it whole!

OCEAN FISHES

218 The world's most venomous fish is the Stonefish. But the venom is used as a defence mechanism. It emits the venom through its dorsal spine when under threat. The stonefish is also a master of disguise. It lies on the coral or rocky reef and looks exactly like its substrate. In some cases, it even has algae growing on it!

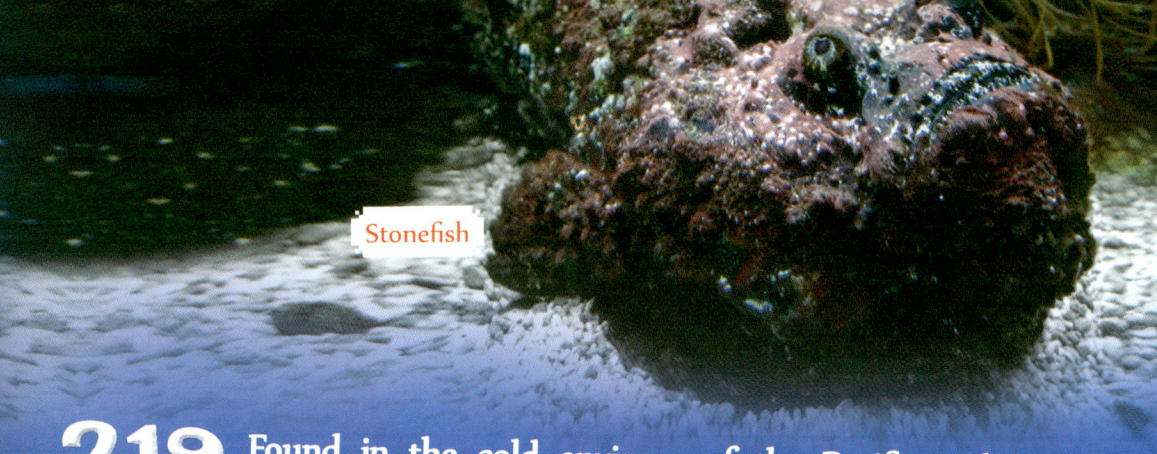

Stonefish

219 Found in the cold environs of the Pacific and Atlantic Oceans, Cod-fish is valued highly as food. It usually stays near the ocean bottom. The size and lifespan of the cod depends on its species. Cods are highly valued as food because they are a rich source of vitamins E, A and D, as well as omega-3 fatty acids.

220 Like many bony fishes, the Swordfish starts out as a tiny larva and then grows rapidly to become one of the largest bony fishes, weighing around 650 kilograms. Some grow by as much as a million times. Perhaps the most distinctive feature of the swordfish is its long, sword-like bill. It uses the sword to stun its prey when hunting.

Swordfish

LIFE IN THE OCEANS

221 **The Sturgeons are one of the oldest fishes on the planet, over 200 million years old!** Native to the Northern Hemisphere, particularly Russia and Ukraine, they live in the sea and travel to rivers each year to lay eggs. Individuals may live for over 100 years. Sturgeons are usually one of the top predators in their habitat.

222 **The Clown Triggerfish gets its name from its bright orange lips that resemble a clown's.** The rest of its body carries equally eye-catching patterns. It has a trick when defending itself from predators. It dives down into a hole in a coral, extends its spine and then bites down on the coral, making it very difficult for a predator to pull out!

223 **The common Clownfish lives among anemones, with which it has a symbiotic relationship.** It has a body covered with mucous that protects it from the anemone's stings. This also gives the clownfish protection from predators who avoid the anemone. In return, the clownfish keeps the anemone clean from parasites.

OCEAN FISHES

224 **There are about 40 species of Triggerfish found across the world.** They live at the bottom of the ocean. They have a unique way of chasing their prey. They dig out burrowing crabs and worms by flapping away the sand and squirting water through their mouth to clear the rest.

225 **The ferocious looking Atlantic Wolffish is a powerful and voracious predator.** It has powerful jaws with large canine teeth that are perfect for eating some of the tough-skinned or spiny sea creatures. Although solitary by nature, males and females usually come together for spawning. Though unusual, they also guard their eggs after laying them.

Sharks and Rays

226 To most of us, Sharks are ferocious creatures that eat up unsuspecting people. But in reality, they rarely attack humans. In fact, sharks belong to a special category among fish, because their skeleton is made entirely of cartilage, rather than bones.

227 The largest predatory fish in the world is the Great White Shark. It is known as a fast, aggressive and intelligent killer. Its muscular body is specially adapted for chasing down its prey in the ocean. Its body temperature is higher than the surrounding water which helps it to move quickly in cold water, especially when hunting warm-blooded marine mammals.

Great White Shark

228 One of the most abundant shark species in the oceans is the Dogfish. It is so named because of its habit of chasing its prey in dog-like packs. But its defining characteristic is the sharp, venomous spines found at each dorsal fin, which makes it a mighty predator.

Dogfish Shark

SHARKS AND RAYS

229 **The Tiger Shark gets its name from the vertical lines seen at the sides of its body.** The lines fade as they reach adulthood. They are aggressive predators who are known to eat anything available, from fish, snakes and birds, to metal, rubber and even garbage. This is why they are called the 'wastebasket of the sea'!

Tiger Shark

230 **The Hammerhead Shark's head does not just gives it its unique name, it also makes it a formidable predator.** It has wide-set eyes which give it a wide visual range. The head of a hammerhead shark has unique sensory organs that help it detect prey, such as ampullae, which allow it to detect a prey's electrical field.

231 **Even though it is not the scariest or biggest shark around, the Bull Shark is probably the most dangerous.** This is because it is very aggressive, likes to stay near crowded coastal areas and does not mind going into freshwater areas. Although humans are not their natural prey, they are most likely to attack one accidentally.

Bull Shark

232 **One of the best cases of camouflage among sharks is seen in the Tasselled Wobbegong.** It gets its name from the branched skin flaps around its mouth that resemble tassels. It has patchy skin which helps it blend into the ocean floor, where it waits motionless for its prey.

LIFE IN THE OCEANS

233 **The strange looking Frilled Shark is also called a 'living fossil' because it seems to have changed very little since prehistoric times.** Its frills are actually its gills that have a red edge, giving it a 'frilly' appearance. They have a serpentine body and swim like a snake or eel. Found in the deep, dark ocean, they are very rarely spotted.

234 **The Whale Shark is over 40 feet long, making it the largest fish in the world.** But despite its massive size, it is one of the gentler shark species. It is a filter feeder and prefers plankton. To eat, it keeps its massive jaws open and filters whatever comes in. These are migratory fish, travelling from the Gulf of Mexico, across the Atlantic and Indian Oceans, to reach the Australian west coast.

235 **Commonly found in coral reefs in tropical regions, the Zebra Shark has a distinctive pattern of black spots with yellowish stripes.** The patterns change as the shark matures. This nocturnal creature has an agile body, ideal for wriggling in and out of coral reefs. It has whiskers and a small mouth that helps it to suck in its prey.

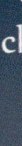

SHARKS AND RAYS

236 Like the shark, the Ray Fish also have a cartilaginous skeleton. The 534 ray species have a flat, disk-like body, wide pectoral fins and a long, slender tail. These marine fish are found in all the oceans. They are divided into three groups: Electric Rays, Sawfishes, and Skates.

237 Electric Rays get their name from their ability to produce electrical shocks. The shock of an electrical ray is strong enough to fell an adult human! It is used for both defence and killing its prey. There are a number of electric ray species. These bottom-dwelling rays are found in warm and temperate ocean waters.

238 Sawfish are shark-like rays which are found in the shallow waters of tropical oceans. These bottom-dwelling rays often swim upriver, with some species even living in freshwater. They get their name from their saw-like snout, which resembles a long, flat blade with a serrated edge. This snout is useful to the ray in digging out the prey from the ocean floor.

LIFE IN THE OCEANS

239 **Unlike other rays, the Skates reproduce by laying eggs.** These eggs have tendrils that get attached to a surface like seaweed. They are found all over the world—from tropical oceans to near-Arctic regions. They have large pectoral fins, making their shape almost round or diamond-shaped.

240 **The Stingray spends most of its time immobile, buried in the seafloor.** Its skin, close to the seafloor's colour, acts as a camouflage. The stingray has sensors around its mouth that helps it to detect the electrical current of its prey. It gets its name from the spines or barbs on its tail, which is highly poisonous.

241 **The Manta Ray has the largest brain among fish.** Unlike other fish, they can also keep their body temperature more or less stable. You will always find them swimming, because they must swim to stay alive! This is because swimming ensures that there is a continuous flow of oxygen-rich water through their body.

SHARKS AND RAYS

242 **The Shovelnose Guitarfish looks like a cross between a ray and a shark.** It has a flattened body with pectoral fins like a ray, with the hind body of a shark. Like all rays, this small-sized fish is found on the ocean floor. It is able to camouflage itself by staying still. It manages to breathe, as it can pump water through its gills while remaining completely motionless!

243 **Eagle Rays have enlarged pectoral fins.** Some eagle ray species also have a sharp-edged serrated tail. They are found in almost all major oceans. Like other rays, they are bottom dwellers and swim along the ocean floor. However, some species are also found closer to the surface, even jumping out sometimes!

244 **The Porcupine Ray gets its name from the sharp thorns on its back.** These act as an excellent defence mechanism in the absence of the poisonous barb that other stingrays carry in their tail.

Eagle Ray

245 **The Cownose Ray gets its name from the shape of its head, which looks like a cow's nose when viewed from the top.** Found in the western Atlantic Ocean, it is an active swimmer like other eagle rays. It has a strong jaw with hard tooth plates. This helps them to chew their favoured prey—hard shelled invertebrates like scallops.

Cownose Ray

Sea Turtles and Reptiles

246 Turtles are reptiles. They are one of the most ancient creatures on the earth, and scientists believe they have existed since the era of dinosaurs. They have a hard shell that protects them from predators. They are aquatic creatures, adapted to life in the sea, even though they come ashore to lay eggs. Did you know, a female turtle always lays its egg at the place she was born!

247 The Leatherback Turtle gets its name from its soft, leathery shell, which is quite unlike the usual hard shell of other turtles. Its shell is composed of a cartilage-like tissue. Weighing up to 900 kilograms, it is the largest turtle on the planet. The leatherback turtle is known to travel great distances, sometimes across oceans, in its journey to its nesting grounds.

SEA TURTLES AND REPTILES

248 **Small in size, the Ridley Sea Turtle is a critically endangered turtle species.** It has an almost circular shell, which is greenish on top with a pale yellow bottom. During nesting season, the female ridley turtles come together and lay their eggs in clutches. These eggs must incubate for 50–60 days before they hatch.

249 **The Loggerhead Turtle gets its name from its broad and strong head.** Together with a powerful jaw, the loggerhead turtle can easily crush tough-shelled invertebrates like the queen conch and lobsters. They mature slowly and live a long life. Like other marine turtles, they travel throughout the ocean and return to their birthplace for nesting.

250 **As the name suggests, the Hawksbill Turtle has a curved, pointed beak like that of a hawk.** Its unique beak helps it to feed underwater on sponges and invertebrates. Unlike other turtles, it is not known for migration, preferring to stay on coral reefs. In addition, hawksbill turtle nests are found in beaches throughout its range.

LIFE IN THE OCEANS

251 **The Green Turtle gets its name not from its shell, but its body.** With a weight of 317.5 kilograms and length up to 5 feet, it is among the largest sea turtles in the world. Unlike other turtles, it is herbivorous and loves the sun. The Eastern Pacific green turtle is often seen coming ashore to sunbathe alongside seals and albatrosses.

252 **There are 55 species of Sea Snakes, and these are highly poisonous.** They are usually found in the warmer and shallower waters of the Indian and Pacific Oceans. They evolved from land snakes, but are now completely adapted to the water, spending their lives in the ocean. However, they cannot breathe underwater and must come out of the water to breathe.

253 **Found in Indian and Pacific Oceans, the Banded Sea Krait is a sea snake.** It has dark bands on its white body. It lives on coral reefs, but unlike some sea snakes it also spends considerable time on land. These snakes come ashore to nest and shed their skin. When they need to hunt, they use a powerful venom to paralyse their victim and swallow it whole.

SEA TURTLES AND REPTILES

254 **The six feet long Olive Sea Snake is found in the waters along northern Australia and nearby islands.** Like a lot of sea snakes, it has large lungs that enable it to hold its breath for a long time when underwater. It has unique light sensing organs in its tail and often spends the entire day hiding in coral reefs.

255 **Like many Galapagos species, the Marine Iguana is special and unique.** It is the only lizard that spends time in the ocean and has adapted itself to island life. It has sharp claws that help it to cling onto rocks, sharp teeth to pull algae from rocks and a flattened tail for rowing in water.

256 **Saltwater Crocodiles are usually found in brackish water in coastal areas.** They are the largest reptiles on earth, growing to over 23 feet in length and 990 kilograms in weight. They have really strong jaws and can hold their breath for a long time. This makes them formidable and clever hunters. Like most reptiles, they come ashore to sunbathe and nest.

Seabirds

257 **Penguins are flightless marine birds that have adapted perfectly to an aquatic life.** For instance, their wing bones are more like flippers, and their sleek bodies are made for swimming and not flying. Most of their life is spent in water, though they do come ashore to bring up their young. Penguins are carnivorous birds.

258 **Adélie penguins start off their aquatic life with extreme reluctance.** They crowd at the edge of the ocean and wait till one of them falls in or is pushed in! Scientists think that this is their way of checking for predators. They are found in Antarctica and feed on small marine creatures like krill and shrimp.

259 **The largest penguin is the Emperor Penguin.** The male and female penguins take turns to care for their young. Immediately after laying eggs, the mothers go into the ocean in search of food, while the fathers take care of the eggs and the newborns. When the mothers return, the fathers go in search of food.

SEABIRDS

260 **The Jackass Penguin gets its name from the peculiar call it makes, which resembles a donkey's call.** They are also called African Penguins, since they are the only penguins found in that continent. They form their nest by digging into seabird droppings that line the coast. They mate for life and take turns to care of their young.

261 **Found on the Galapagos islands, the Galapagos penguin is one of the temperate penguins and the only one that is found around the equator.** It also makes these penguins quite unique. With a more hospitable climate, they breed round the year. Like many other penguins, they mate for life and take care of their young.

262 **The Rockhopper Penguins get their name from their ability to hop or bound over rocks unlike their waddling brethren.** At less than two feet, they are quite short. But they have a very distinctive physical appearance, with blood-red eyes, an orange beak, pink webbed feet and a crest of spiky yellow feathers at the outer edge of their eyebrows.

LIFE IN THE OCEANS

263 The small, slender Arctic Tern are known for their long migrations, from one pole to another. In fact, no other species on earth travels such great distances in its lifetime. The arctic tern is known for its geographical range. It nests in the Arctic, but migrates across the world to the Antarctic in the winter.

264 The Atlantic Puffin lives in the Atlantic Ocean and like other seabirds, it is completely adapted to sea life. It can dive underwater using its wings. But puffins are also good fliers and will often fly long distances when nesting. The atlantic puffin comes ashore to nest in colonies with other nesting pairs.

265 The iconic Bald Eagle, a symbol of the United States, is an impressive bird of prey. It is found along the North American coastline, preferring both freshwater and marine fish for food. It is an impressive predator, even feeding on other birds. It is equally likely to scavenge for a meal, or even steal from other predators.

SEABIRDS

266 **There are more than 20 species of Seagulls found all over the planet including at the two poles.** They are noisy birds that prefer to live in colonies that range from a few birds to thousands. Seagulls have a big diet, feeding on plants and worms as well as amphibians. They are even known to eat their own young!

267 **At nearly two feet tall, the European Herring Gull is among the largest of its species.** It is found at the North Atlantic coast of Europe and Western Asia. Although it is a predator, it also scavenges for food, and human garbage is one of its main sources of food. It has been known to attack other nests and feed on eggs and juveniles.

268 **The Laughing Gull gets its name from its high-pitched laugh.** It has a white body with grey wings and a black head. The colour of the head changes to a subtle grey in winter. Like other gulls, it both hunts and scavenges for its food. Unlike many other gulls, however, it is found only in the coastal areas.

LIFE IN THE OCEANS

269 The Pelican is characterised by a pouch in its throat. The pouch is used for catching fish. They often swim in a U-shaped formation or in a line. This is not for show, though. By swimming together in this formation and flapping their wings, they force the fish into shallow water, where they are easy to scoop up!

270 One of the most well-known Pelican, found in the Gulf of Mexico. Unlike other pelicans, it feeds by plunge-diving into the water and scooping out large mouthfuls of water which could contain both fish and other seafood. These birds usually stick close to the shore, but can also glide over large distances.

271 An Albatross has the longest wingspan of any bird, up to 11 feet. These massive wings enable the Albatross to glide for hours without flapping their wings much. They can also float on the ocean surface. They drink saltwater and feed on squid and schools of fish. Albatross often follow ships in the hope of finding food.

SEABIRDS

272
Despite a wingspan of nearly seven feet, the Laysan Albatross is relatively smaller than other albatrosses. Like other albatrosses, it is a graceful flier. But on land it is noticeably clumsier! It breeds in large colonies in the Northwestern Hawaiian Islands. The laysan albatross mates for life and has a strong pair bond.

273 The Osprey is sometimes confused with the bald eagle because of its appearance and its ability to swoop from a height (almost 100 feet) and pluck its catch from the water. In fact, it is known to get into fights with eagles mid-air to save its catch! It is a migratory bird, nesting in the north and travelling south in winters.

LIFE IN THE OCEANS

274 The magnificent Frigate Bird is a truly magnificent bird with one of the largest wingspans among seabirds. Unlike other seabirds, it cannot fly when wet. Hence, it has devised interesting alternative methods of catching its prey, such as stealing from other seabirds. Frigate birds are also extremely adept at catching sea creatures like squid and flying fish when they leap out of the water.

275 There are around 40 species of Cormorants. Individual species can vary widely, but all of them are excellent divers. When underwater, they use their wings as rudders and their webbed feet for speed. This also means that they have small wings. They have oil-secreting glands that keep their feathers waterproof to some extent.

Marine Algae and Plants

276 **As on land, the ocean food chain too is based on chlorophyll-bearing organisms like plants and algae.** The algae are often at the bottom of the food chain in the ocean. Where the ocean meets the land, we often find different kinds of marine plants like sea palm and mangrove trees.

277 **The oceans are rich in plant life.** As we go down deeper into the ocean we find varied and abundant plants, like seagrass and kelp. Although these are anchored on the ocean floor, they grow towards the surface, their leaves thick and fibrous. We also find phytoplankton and algae sticking to rocks, corals and other creatures.

278 Algae are marine organisms that use photosynthesis to produce oxygen, just like plants. However, they do not have roots, stems, leaves or a vascular system. Algae are neither plants nor animals. They belong to a group called protists. You are probably familiar with some types of algae-like pond scum that floats on top of the ponds, or seaweed.

LIFE IN THE OCEANS

279

Algae are a diverse group, with 27,000 different species, that range from single-celled to multi-cellular organisms. Most algae can live independently, but some form symbiotic relationships with different organisms. Most algae are found in water—oceans, ponds and rivers—but some are also land-dwelling. Some are even found in animal fur!

280

Algae offer an important food base for all aquatic life. But more importantly, it has played a vital role in creating the earth's ecosystem. Algae's ability to generate oxygen through photosynthesis is extremely important in sustaining life on earth. Did you know, algae are an important source for crude oil, certain medicines and industrial products.

MARINE ALGAE AND PLANTS

Lichens on a branch.

281

Many species of algae develop a symbiotic relationship with other organisms. Typically, algae provide food through photosynthesis, while the other organisms offer defence and protection. Examples include lichens, which are a combination of algae and fungi. In coral reefs, algae provide food through photosynthesis, while the coral provides it with nutrition and protection.

282
Marine algae are also known as seaweed. There are three kinds of algae: Green Algae, Red Algae and Brown Algae. Brown algae are found in temperate or Arctic water. Red algae are found at great depths. They can survive in the difficult conditions in the deep sea because of their ability to absorb blue light. Green algae thrive in any moist environment, including the sea, freshwater and even moist soil.

283
Green Algae are found near the water surface, often attached to a rocky substrate. Because of their green colour, the green algae seem most plant-like. But unlike plants, they lack a vascular system that would carry water from roots to the leaves. As the algae live in the water, liquid passes directly to their cells.

LIFE IN THE OCEANS

284 The Green Algae are found in all marine regions, even in rather inhospitable conditions. These hardy algae come in all shapes and sizes. For instance, Caulerpa prolifera, found on some coastal seafloors is actually the largest one-celled organism in the world. One form of green algae, Enteromorpha, live in conditions that would not suit most plants or algae, like extreme temperature and moisture.

285 A commonly found green algae is the Sea Lettuce. It gets its name from its lobed, sheet-like structure that resembles a lettuce. It has no stalks or roots, although some of them may have a root-like structure called holdfast. Interestingly, it thrives in water with high pollution. Hence, it is often used as an indicator of pollution level!

286 The Brown Algae gets its colour from a mixture of pigments in its cells—the green pigment chlorophyll and the yellow pigment xanthophyll. This mix of pigments gives the brown algae a range in their colouration. Brown algae are very useful, as they provide nutrition and shelter to other organisms. They are also used by humans as a source of food.

MARINE ALGAE AND PLANTS

287 Although algae do not have roots, some species like the Brown Algae Fucus have a tough tissue called a holdfast that acts like roots, which helps the algae cling to rocks, thereby preventing them from floating away. On the other hand, the brown algae like Sargassum float on the ocean surface like a mat.

288 The largest marine 'plant' is actually the brown algae named Kelp. Some kelp species like the giant kelp can grow as large as 250 metres! Usually found in cold coastal water, it has small floating bulbs that help keep it afloat. They can form dense forests that support entire ecosystems!

LIFE IN THE OCEANS

Red Seaweed

289 Red Algae form the most abundant of algae species, with more than 7,000 kinds known to us! It carries the red pigment, phycoerythrin and the blue pigment, phycocyanin. The two pigments give it the vivid colour and enable it to use the limited light available in the deep ocean to carry out photosynthesis.

Jamaican Irish Moss

290 Red Algae are not just eaten by different marine creatures, they are also eaten widely by people. The flat, sheet-like nori, the bushy Irish moss and agar, carrageenan producing algae are all used by humans as food. The algae come in many textures. Some algae are thin and delicate, while some are hard and brittle.

291 Unlike seaweed, the Seagrass is a flowing plant. It is found in oceans in temperate and tropical regions. Like the grass on land, the seagrass is also long, thin and narrow. Found in shallow waters, it can grow in patches (in wavy regions) or as a thick carpet (in calm waters).

MARINE ALGAE AND PLANTS

292 **There are many plants found at the beaches.** Interestingly, you will find plants only at the upper beaches because the constant flow of salty water, tides and surf makes it impossible for plants to grow on lower beaches. The plants on the upper beach serve their own purpose. Their roots hold together the sand dunes on the beach, preventing it from getting washed away.

293 **Beach plants are a peculiar breed.** Only specially adapted plants can thrive in the loose, shifty, salty sand with little freshwater. Because of their specific adaptations, these plants find it impossible to survive in other places. Like desert plants, these plants are adapted to scarce water conditions. They grow close to the ground, spreading out with strong roots and succulent leaves that hold moisture.

LIFE IN THE OCEANS

294 The Red Sand verbena, native to California, is the perfect example of beach adaption. It is found on sand dunes at the beach, near the ocean surf. It needs saline water to survive, which it gets in the form of sea spray. It is a succulent plant, storing salt in its tissues. It is a rare species and provides shelter to many small organisms.

Red Sand Verbena

Pampas Grass is considered an unwanted, invasive weed in many areas.

295 Named after its native region, Pampas in South America, the Pampas grass was introduced to North America and Europe as a means of controlling erosion. This highly adaptable grass thrives in coastal sand dunes, marshes and shrublands. This tall, slender grass grows in dense tussocks. Each blade of grass produces millions of seeds, spreading quickly and easily.

Mangrove Forests

296 Found in the tropical and subtropical regions, Mangrove forests grow in coastal or brackish water. They are easily recognisable because of their dense formation with, the roots jutting out of the water. These trees are adapted to the harsh conditions of their habitat. The roots have a complex salt filtration system and can withstand waterlogging.

MARINE ALGAE AND PLANTS

297 Sea Oats grow slowly, but live a fairly long life. This perennial grass is found on upper beaches where it thrives in the coarse or medium grained sediments and blowing sand. It has a massive root system and can tolerate a brief deluge of saltwater. It cannot survive on lower beaches that are wetter and more fine-grained.

298 The Sea Palm is a brown algae found on the western coast of North America. It is found in patches of a few algae to a few thousand! It is a kelp species, the only one that can stand upright in air without water. It is often found on shores, with strong waves, where most other plants would not survive.

The oil from the punna plant are considered beneficial in Ayurvedic medicine.

LIFE IN THE OCEANS

299 While many marine plants are eaten around the world, some of them have multiple benefits. Punna, found in the coastal regions of India, is known for its medicinal properties. The oil extracted from its seed is anti-inflammatory. It is used for relieving pain, rheumatism and in arthritis treatment. It is an evergreen plant that is highly adaptable.

300 The ocean and its coast are full of life in different forms. There are psychedelic invertebrates, giant mammals, ancient creatures and sturdy plants. Marine life is remarkable for its adaption and sheer variety. Interestingly, we still know very little about life in our oceans. But as we go forward in our journey, who knows the mysteries we will uncover!

OCEAN ECOSYSTEMS

Coral Reefs

301 The ocean is like an entire universe in itself with multiple ecosystems co-existing. An ecosystem is a community where many species live together. The ecosystem provides them with a habitat and other non-living support systems, like air and water. The unique ecosystems found undersea give us unique organisms and a rich ocean life.

302 Coral reefs are not just one of the most thriving marine ecosystems, they are also one of the most prolific on earth. In fact, they are nicknamed the 'rainforests of the sea'. Like rainforests on land, they are home to more than a million species. In fact, many coral reef scientists are still discovering new species living in coral reefs!

303 Although coral reefs cover less than one per cent of the earth's surface (less than two per cent of the ocean floor), almost a quarter of all the ocean species depend on these reefs for food and shelter. Not just that, the life here is also incredibly diverse. For instance, the Northwestern Hawaiian Island coral reefs support more than 7,000 diverse species!

OCEAN ECOSYSTEMS

304 **Did you know that coral reefs are alive?** They may look like rocks, but these are live organisms! In fact, many of them attach themselves to the seafloor through 'roots'. So, are they plants? No. Since they cannot produce their own food, they are not plants either. In fact, they are animals, and often eat organisms that float by!

305 **A coral mound consists of many tiny animals called polyps.** Some of these polyps are very small, while some can be as big as a foot in diameter. They are invertebrates, closely related to anemones and jellyfish. Some polyps live individually (such as the mushroom corals), while some live in large colonies, forming reef structures.

306 **A polyp has a sac-like body with a mouth encircled by stinging tentacles.** It uses carbonate and calcium from the seawater to build itself a hard, cup-shaped skeleton. It builds multiple skeletons, which later form a sectional structure, that protects its soft body. Polyps use their tentacles to capture small organisms like planktons that float too close.

CORAL REEFS

307 **The polyp skeleton is white, like most animals.** However, most of them have a clear body. So, where do the polyps get their brilliant colouration? The colour comes from the millions of tiny algae that live in the polyp tissues! These algae have a brilliant pigment that is visible through the polyp's clear body.

308 **The relationship between the polyps and algae is perfectly symbiotic.** The algae get shelter and use the coral's metabolic waste for photosynthesis. The corals, in turn, benefit from the oxygen produced and waste removed by the algae. This partnership has ensured that coral reefs are some of the oldest, thriving, ecologically diverse communities on the planet.

309 **Not all corals are hard. Some corals, like sea fans, are known as soft corals because of their soft, flexible bodies.** But coral reefs are built by hard corals whose polyps create a hard calcium carbonate skeleton. Like other animals, corals also reproduce and many of them prefer to live in colonies. Together these colonies become reefs.

OCEAN ECOSYSTEMS

310 Reef building corals come in a wide range of shapes, accounting for the diversity of reef structures. For instance, branching corals actually have 'branches', while table corals form table-like structures. Encrusting corals grow as a thin layer and elkhorn coral have thick branches that resemble an elk's antlers!

311 Even through polyps are tiny organisms, they can build colonies and reefs that stretch over miles! But colonies take time to build and therefore, some reefs are thousands of years old. The Great Barrier Reef in Australia is at least 20,000 years old! The long life and slow building process is possible because the polyps grow and reproduce slowly.

312 Coral reefs are classified into three types: fringe reef, barrier reef and atoll. Fringe reefs grow close to the shoreline, while barrier reefs grow at a little distance from the shoreline. An atoll starts life as a fringe reef around a volcanic island. When the island sinks, the coral completely takes over, covering the area and forming an atoll.

CORAL REEFS

313 **The fringe reef, also known as shore reef, is the most commonly found reef structure in the world.** Since it grows adjacent to land, it is also most susceptible to pollution. In some cases, a fringing reef may grow at a slight distance, with back reef areas covered in seagrass meadows. Examples of this kind of reef are found in the Caribbean, Bahamas and Red Sea.

314 **The best example of the barrier reef is the Great Barrier Reef off the coast of Queensland, Australia.** Stretching over 344,400 square kilometres, composed of more than 2,900 individual reefs, the Great Barrier Reef is the largest coral reef system on the planet. So vast is its expanse that you can actually see it from the outer space!

315 **The Great Barrier Reef is considered one of the wonders of the natural world because of the richness of its ecosystem.** Apart from more than 400 corals found here, the reef supports sponges, invertebrates, more than 1,500 fish species and 200 bird species, reptiles and sea turtles. It is also the breeding ground for humpback whales.

OCEAN ECOSYSTEMS

316 Atolls are usually found in the South Pacific and Indian Oceans. This is possibly because these regions had numerous volcanic islands that later sank into the ocean floor. An example of an atoll is the Maldives. Did you know, this classification was first devised by Charles Darwin, who saw this as an evolutionary passage! Thus, reefs start off as fringe reefs, become barrier reefs and finally evolve into atolls.

317 Where do we find coral reefs? Corals need clear and highly saline water that allows light to pass through. Corals don't grow well in murky, deep, dark waters. This is because the algae in the coral polyps need these conditions for photosynthesis. Hence, corals are found only in shallow tropical and subtropical waters.

318 You can think of coral reefs as cities where many animals, fish and even birds live. In fact, many of the organisms on the coral reefs have symbiotic relationships with each other. One frequent inhabitant is the sea sponge that you can find in all shapes and sizes on corals. They in turn provide shelter to smaller creatures, like crabs and shrimps.

CORAL REEFS

319 **Sea anemones on corals have symbiotic relationships with clownfish and anemone fish.** The anemone's tentacles provide protection and shelter for these fish and their eggs. In return, anemone fish protects the anemone from predators and parasites. The microscopic invertebrate Bryozoans form colonies over coral skeletons, cementing its structure.

320 **Fish are important residents or neighbours of coral reefs.** Predators like sharks live close by, eating smaller fish, while eels live within the coral structure. These predators are important in keeping a check on the coral population. Some cleaner fishes clean the area. Other fish share a symbiotic relationship with corals.

OCEAN ECOSYSTEMS

321 Not all fish and animals have a great relationship with corals. Some are avid predators, such as some fish species, snails, worms and sea stars. One particularly dangerous predator is the crown-of-thorns sea star. In parts of the Pacific Ocean, population explosion of this star has resulted in widescale destruction of coral reefs.

322 Apart from predators, corals reefs face threat from many other sources, both natural and man-made. Increased exposure due to prolonged low tide, rising salinity and strong, powerful hurricanes and storms can severely damage coral reefs. While they can recover in some cases, a prolonged threat can cause irreparable damage.

CORAL REEFS

323 **Unfortunately, human activities have added to this threat.** Overfishing and coral hunting has directly and drastically reduced the coral population. In some cases, pollution has caused the rise of invasive species that damage the corals. In addition, rising water temperature and ocean acidification have caused severe damage to coral colonies. Highly acidified seawater damages existing structures and makes it difficult for coral to rebuild their skeleton.

324 **When corals are under threat, the polyps go into stress.** The stressed polyps then eject the resident algae that produce their food. Since the algae also provide them with colour, these stressed polyps turn white. This process is called coral bleaching. Bleached corals are more likely to die of starvation or disease.

325 **The biodiversity of coral reefs is not the only reason they are important.** Fish and other animals that live around reefs provide an important source of food for people. The corals are also important tourist attractions, providing employment to many in the coastal community. Not just that, many scientists are now using corals to develop medicine!

Deep Hydrothermal Vents

326 **In 1977, a group of marine geologists exploring the Galápagos Rift in the Eastern Pacific noticed a sudden rise in temperature.** This was very surprising, since in deep-ocean, temperatures nearby were near freezing. Then, they discovered deep vents in the ocean floor. These were deep-sea hydrothermal vents. They also realised that these vents created a site for entirely unique ecosystems!

327 **The deep, dark ocean with its extremes of pressures and temperatures, toxic minerals, and lack of sunlight may seem completely inhospitable.** Yet, it houses hundreds of fascinating species. The geologists who discovered the hydrothermal vents realised that these species flourished around these vents.

328 **Today we know that deep hydrothermal vents are located in all the oceans.** They are found in areas that show high tectonic activity, such as tectonic plate edges, undersea mountain ranges and mid-ocean ridges. You can think of them as hot springs or geysers. Interestingly, hydrothermal vents were found on the moons of both Jupiter and Saturn, and may even have existed on Mars!

DEEP HYDROTHERMAL VENTS

329 The creation of deep hydrothermal vents shows us how the earth is constantly changing, as its tectonic plates are always in motion. We typically find the hydrothermal vents along the mid-ocean ridge where the tectonic plates are spreading apart. At these places, the underlying magma rises up and then cools down to form a new crust.

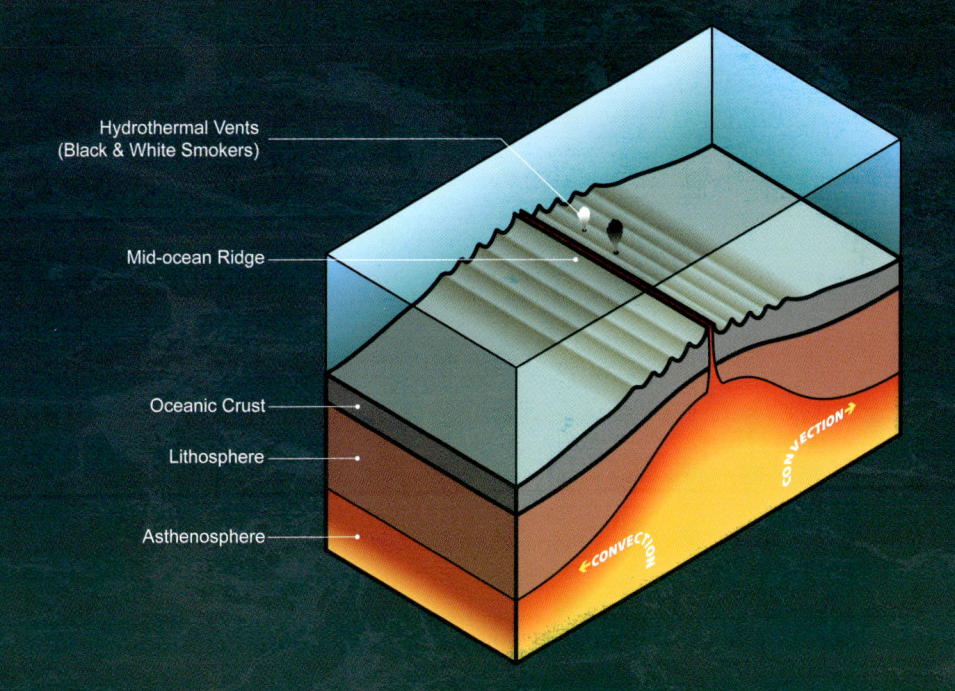

- Hydrothermal Vents (Black & White Smokers)
- Mid-ocean Ridge
- Oceanic Crust
- Lithosphere
- Asthenosphere

330 Seawater that trickles down into the ocean's crust through fissures and vents, becomes super-hot due to its contact with hot magma. This super-hot water begins to dissolve minerals around it. As the pressure builds, it rises toward the surface of the crust. Eventually, this hot, mineral-rich water exits the oceanic crust in the form of a geyser.

OCEAN ECOSYSTEMS

331 **The dissolved minerals and metals in the erupting water precipitate when it comes into contact with the cold seawater around it, forming a vent.** Although the temperature of the seawater in hydrothermal vents can reach over 400°C, the hot seawater does not come to a boil because of the extreme pressure at that depth!

332 **Deep hydrothermal vents are classified into two kinds: black smoker and white smoker.** The black smokers are typically found in the abyssal zones and even deeper trenches, near spreading tectonic plates. They get their name from the cloud of black material coming out of the ground at that point, through chimney-like structures. Because of their location, they are also known as deep-sea vents.

333 **Black smokers typically release sulfur-bearing minerals or sulfides.** Apart from sulphides, the water is rich in other dissolved minerals as well, like iron. Together they form iron monosulfide which on contact with cold ocean water, precipitates to form a black, chimney-like structure. With its rich sulphide extracts, the deposits around the vent develop substantial sulfide ore deposits with time.

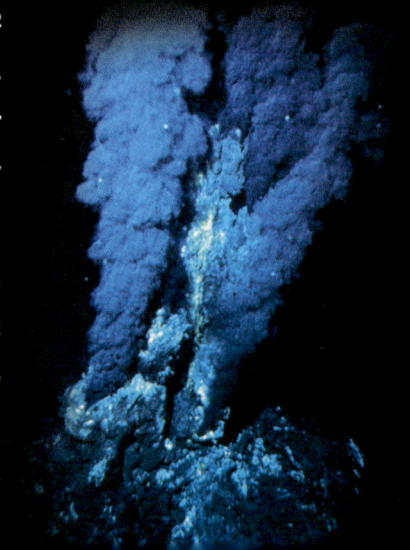

DEEP HYDROTHERMAL VENTS

334 **White smoker vents get their name because they release lighter coloured minerals.** They release minerals containing barium, calcium and silicon. They are also typically not as hot as black smokers because they are usually located at a distance from their heat source. Black smokers are hotter and found more commonly.

335 **There are some vents with even cooler and weaker flows. These are called cold seeps.** They carry gases like hydrogen sulphide and methane. The gases and the difference in temperature gives them a shimmery appearance. They form brine pools, where the salinity of the water is higher than the surrounding water. Over time, cold seep reactions may also form carbonate rocks and reefs.

OCEAN ECOSYSTEMS

336 On the ocean's upper layers, the algae that use sunlight to create food, form the base of the food chain. But the deep ocean floor has no sunlight and no food percolates down. So, how can life exist? For a very long time, scientists believed that life on the ocean floor was either non-existent or extremely sparse.

337 The scientists who discovered the deep hydrothermal vents were shocked to find thriving ecosystems around it. They found that the density of organisms near the vents was almost a thousand times more than the water nearby! So, can you guess why life thrives around the hydrothermal vents under such impossible conditions? The answer lies in the plume of cloudy water it ejects.

338 The water from the hydrothermal vent is rich in dissolved minerals. Although some of these minerals, such as hydrogen sulfide, are highly toxic to most known organisms, they are vital for certain bacteria known as chemoautotrophic bacteria. These bacteria use the chemicals in a process called chemosynthesis to produce organic material.

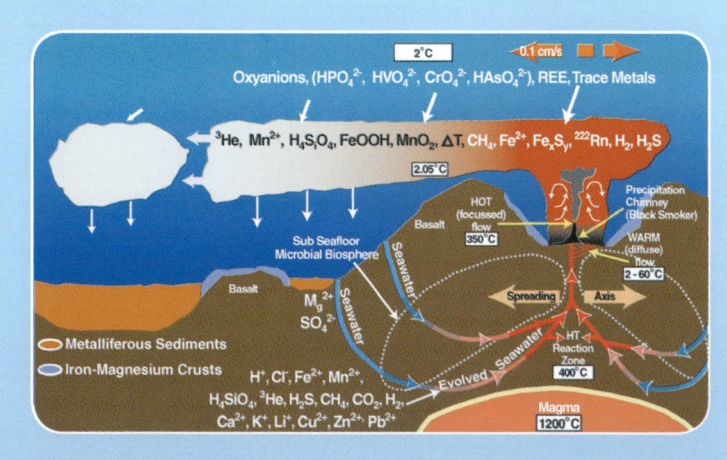

DEEP HYDROTHERMAL VENTS

339 Just as photosynthetic algae and plants form the base of food chain elsewhere, the chemoautotrophic bacteria form the base of the food chain in the deep ocean. The bacteria form a thick mat near the vents on the ocean floor, providing food for smaller organisms, which in turn form the food source for larger organisms like shrimps, crabs and octopuses.

340 The deep hydrothermal vents provide a completely different view to the way we see life elsewhere. Before life was discovered at this depth, we believed that solar energy was the basis of all life on earth. But here, it is hydrogen sulfide that forms the essential element for life! In fact, other chemicals, toxic to most living organisms, sustain life at this depth.

OCEAN ECOSYSTEMS

341 With such unique life conditions, the organisms of the deep ocean also show some special adaptations. In fact, they are some of the most bizarre and unique organisms found anywhere on earth. They have learnt to live in extreme temperatures reaching up to 113°C, extreme pressure and the presence of toxic gases.

342 Scientists have so far found over 300 species in deep hydrothermal vent ecosystems. Most of these—over 95 per cent—were completely unique and unknown before that. With their unique adaptations, they are also found almost exclusively in vent ecosystems. Interestingly, most of these are also believed to be extremely ancient life forms, leading scientists to believe that this is perhaps how life began!

343 One of the unique creatures found here is the Giant Tube Worm. It lives in a tube, reaching up to the height of two metres, which protects its soft body. The red-tipped tube worm hosts chemoautotrophic bacteria, which helps it to derive nutrition from the sulphide-rich environment. Growing in colonies, the giant tube worm is the dominant species in the vent ecosystems.

DEEP HYDROTHERMAL VENTS

344 Researchers who have studied deep-sea creatures, term these ecosystems as an 'evolutionary wonderland' because of the unique adaptations of organisms at this level. Even familiar organisms develop strange features, such as shrimps which often develop 'eyes' on their backs that can sense infrared light! This is probably because they can see the faint light from the vents.

345 Because of the difficulty in reaching this terrain, we still know very little about the deep hydrothermal vent ecosystems. Scientists view them as an important clue in understanding the beginning of life on earth because they believe that primitive earth had similar environmental conditions. But above all, they are proof of the sheer variety and tenacity of life.

Kelp Forests

346 **Did you know that there are forests under the sea?** If the coral reefs are like cities, the kelp forests are the woodlands of our oceans. Like coral reefs, kelp forests form a vital underwater ecosystem that houses thousands of invertebrates, fishes and other ocean inhabitants. These forests are an important breeding ground for many of them.

347 **Although they look like plants, kelps are actually brown algae.** In fact, they also share another important characteristic with plants—kelps can produce their own food using photosynthesis! Together with other seaweeds, kelps are an important part of the marine food web.

348 **There are around 30 different species of kelp.** These algae grow in colonies, creating 'forests' underwater. Smaller colonies are known as kelp beds. These fast growing algae can grow up to 18 inches in a single day and some species can grow as tall as 150 feet! Because of this incredible rate of growth, they can quickly spread over an area.

KELP FORESTS

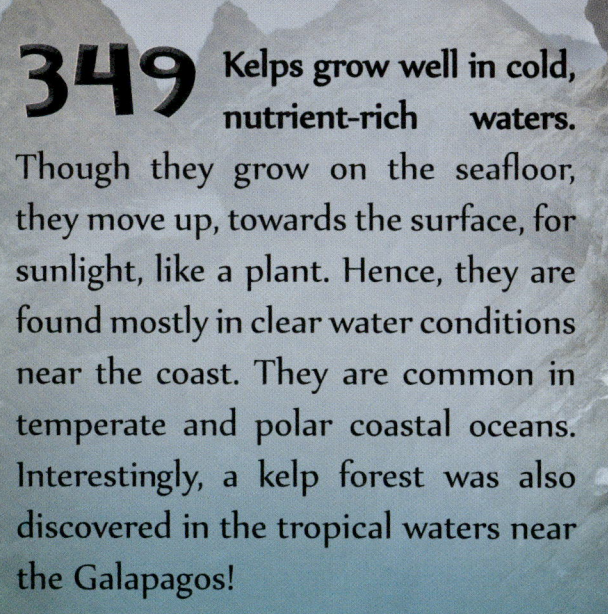

349
Kelps grow well in cold, nutrient-rich waters. Though they grow on the seafloor, they move up, towards the surface, for sunlight, like a plant. Hence, they are found mostly in clear water conditions near the coast. They are common in temperate and polar coastal oceans. Interestingly, a kelp forest was also discovered in the tropical waters near the Galapagos!

350
The kelp's body is usually divided into three parts, just like plants: the root-like holdfast, stalk-like stipe, and the leaf-like fronds. Just like leaves, the fronds grow from the stipe and are the main site for photosynthesis. The holdfast may anchor the kelp, but unlike the roots, it plays no role in absorption of nutrients.

Fronds of brown stalked kelp.

OCEAN ECOSYSTEMS

351 Do you know how kelp stay buoyant and upright? Some kelp species have gas-filled sacs, located at a frond's base. The air in the sacs gives the kelp its buoyancy and keeps the fronds and stipes upright. The number of sacs can vary. While a giant kelp has one at the base of each blade, a bull kelp plant has only one sac to support multiple fronds.

352 Although it does not take its nutrient from the ground or substrate, the kelp does need a suitable substrate to survive. A strong substrate like a large rock helps it to weather storms and other disturbances. In fact, scientists have observed that the stronger the substrate, better are the kelp's chances to stay upright.

353 Kelp forests offer important and highly dynamic ecosystems in the ocean. Unlike coral reefs or mangrove forests, they grow and spread quickly. They are home to a number of marine species. Their ability to provide food and energy to their inhabitants is another remarkable factor in creating entire ecosystems.

KELP FORESTS

354 The structure of the kelp itself makes it appropriate as an 'ecosystem architect'. From the holdfast to the stipe and fronds—each part of the kelp plays a role in building the ecosystem. For instance, the holdfast structure with its nooks and crannies is the perfect home for small creatures. It gives them shelter and protection.

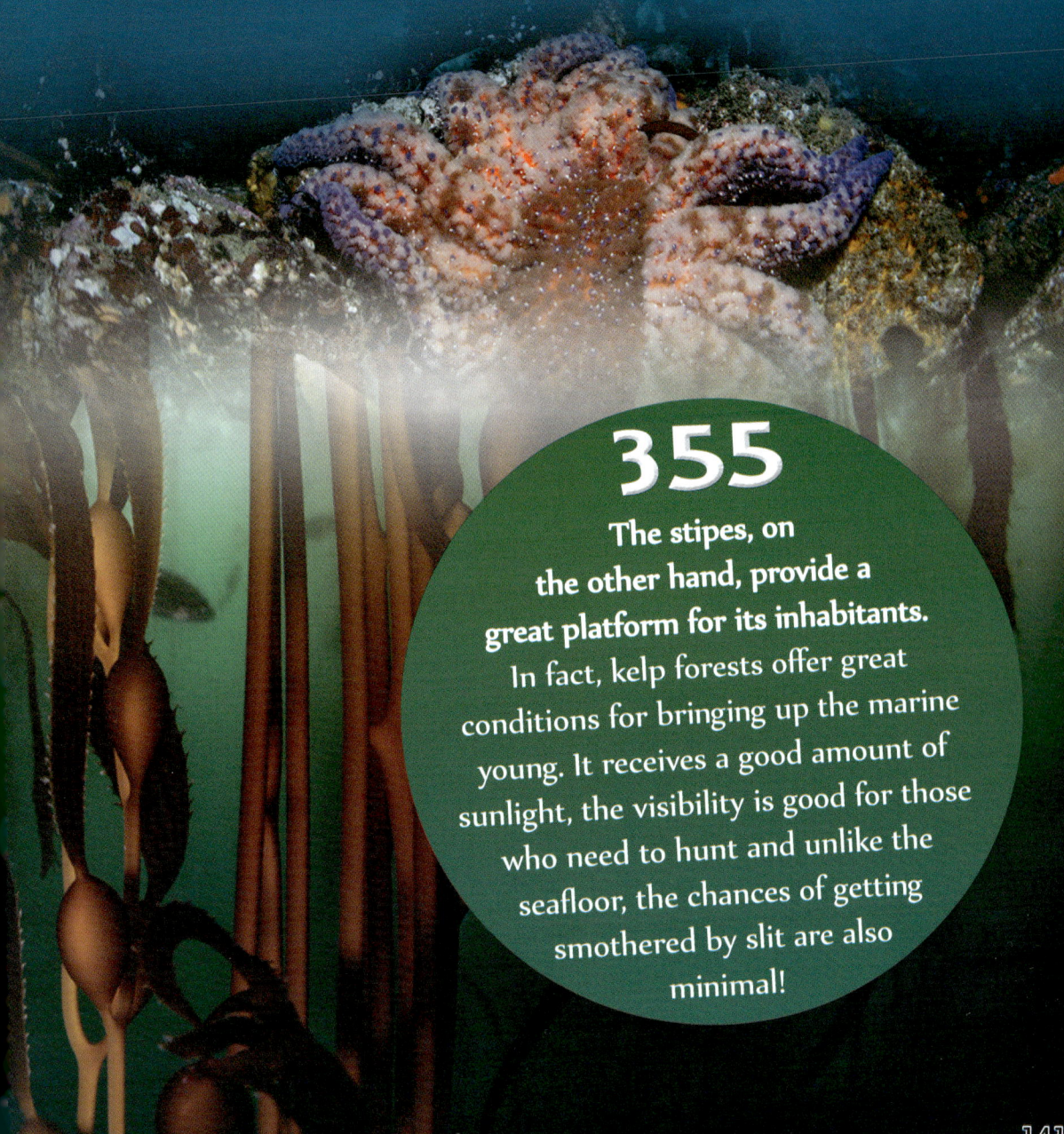

355 The stipes, on the other hand, provide a great platform for its inhabitants. In fact, kelp forests offer great conditions for bringing up the marine young. It receives a good amount of sunlight, the visibility is good for those who need to hunt and unlike the seafloor, the chances of getting smothered by slit are also minimal!

OCEAN ECOSYSTEMS

356 **The fronds also play an important role.** Like the stipe, they provide an excellent platform and shelter for different species. In addition, they are also responsible for the process of photosynthesis. As an important food source, kelp attracts many other species, which in turn attract bigger predatory species.

357 **The kelp ecosystem is fairly complex. It is a mix of different kelp species as well as other algae.** Canopy kelps are usually the largest species. They get their name from the floating canopies they form. Prostrate kelps, on the other hand, lie along the seafloor. The tall stipitate kelps grow in dense colonies.

358 **In addition to kelp, these underground forests also have different algal species at the ocean floor.** Together with the different kelp species, the algae make the kelp forest a dynamic environment, very similar to terrestrial forests. Here, we find a sunlit canopy, a shaded middle area and a dense ocean floor.

KELP FORESTS

359 Kelp forests are not just important as a marine ecosystem, they are also useful in numerous other ways for humans. They are habitat to many commercially important fishes, such as crayfish. Kelp that gets washed up on beaches is equally important. It is used for production of fertilizer and cosmetics.

Kelp is considered a very healthy food.

360 Like other ecosystems, kelp forests are also under threat. One of the natural threats they face is from invasive species like the sea urchin. The sea urchin can destroy kelp forests in a matter of days. Interestingly, there is an easy solution for this. The sea otter preys on the sea urchin, keeping a check on its population!

A male sea otter is seen cleaning his fur with kelp.

361 One of the most critical threats to the kelp ecosystem is the rising global temperature, including in the oceans. Since kelp prefers colder waters, scientists fear that a rise in temperatures can cause drastic changes in their spread. It is suggested that kelp forests near the shores may die or move deeper in the ocean.

Kelp washed up on a beach.

Mangrove Forests

362 Mangroves are small trees that grow on the edges of oceans or seas. At first glance, they may seem like any other forest, only with a bit more water at the bottom! But mangroves are gritty survivors, one of the marvels of nature that teach us how life can survive and thrive even when it seems impossible.

363 Mangroves are the only trees that thrive in saltwater. They grow in areas with low oxygen soil and saline water, in waterlogged mud—conditions that would spell the death knell for most plants! This adaptation allows them to grow in brackish or saline water. Not just that, they also provide a thriving ecosystem in an otherwise harsh intertidal zone.

364 Mangroves can survive in cold conditions, but can't survive so well in frost. They are found in tropical and subtropical regions, mostly close to the equator. Notable mangrove forests are found in Malaysia and Indonesia. According to data collected in 2000, the total area covered by mangrove forests was 137,800 square kilometres, located in 118 territories.

MANGROVE FORESTS

365

Interestingly, mangrove trees are freshwater trees! Do you know how a mangrove grows in an environment that is toxic for any freshwater plant? The answer lies in their unique adaptations. These plants have adapted themselves to deal with low oxygen conditions, waterlogged soil and salinity by filtering what they can take in and using it wisely!

366
The roots of a mangrove tree play an important role and helps it to filter out salt and stay upright. The roots have a complex filtration system, which uses negative pressure to push out the salt from water. Some species filter out as much as 97 per cent of the salt from the water right at the roots!

367
Did you know that if you licked the leaf of a mangrove tree, it will taste salty? This is because the leaves are covered in dried salt crystals! The leaves are the second part of the tree's saltwater adaption. Some mangrove species have special glands in their leaves that excrete salt.

OCEAN ECOSYSTEMS

368 **Since mangroves are freshwater trees, they also hoard the little freshwater they receive.** This means storing as much as they can, while reducing any water loss. The leaves come to their rescue once again. Their waxy succulent leaves are meant to store water. The leaves restrict their stomata (openings) to reduce water loss!

369 **Like the leaves, the roots of the mangrove tree can also multitask!** The exposed roots contain breathing tubes that help the plants to 'breathe' in the low oxygen level of the waterlogged mud. The aerial roots with their wide span keep the plant upright in changing tides and soft, loose soil.

370 **These clever plants also have clever seeds!** In some species, the seeds germinate while still on the parent tree, where they are nourished for a year or two. They are ready to take root wherever they fall. The seeds of the mangrove tree are buoyant. So, if they fall during high tide, they can stay afloat till they find soil to settle down!

A mangrove flower blooming in a mangroves forest in Malaysia.

MANGROVE FORESTS

371 Mangrove seeds are also excellent travellers. The fruits, seeds and seedling can all stay afloat. The seeds can stay dormant and germinate when they reach suitable ground. Both the seedling and seed float in a horizontal position, but as soon as they reach brackish water, they turn vertical, ready to lay down their roots!

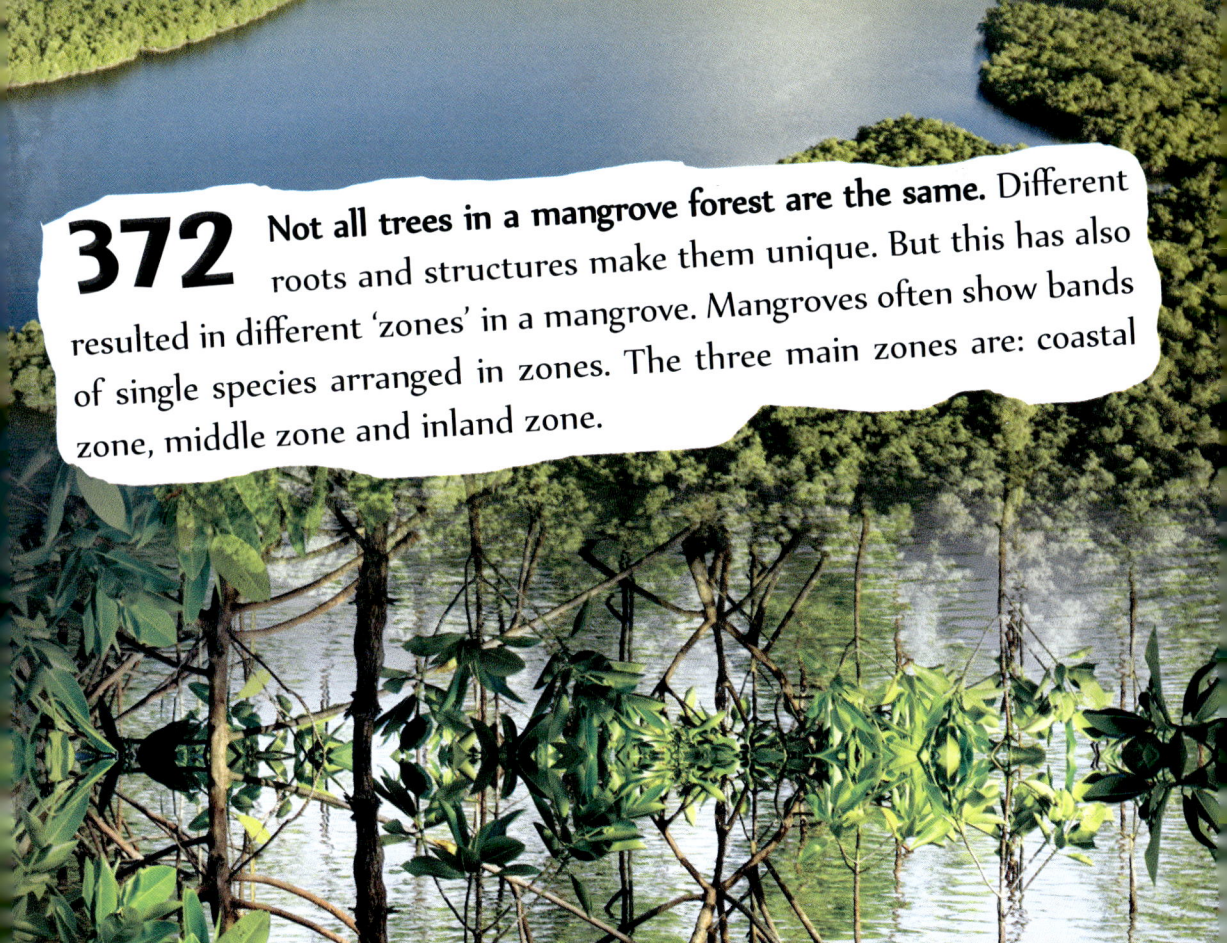

372 Not all trees in a mangrove forest are the same. Different roots and structures make them unique. But this has also resulted in different 'zones' in a mangrove. Mangroves often show bands of single species arranged in zones. The three main zones are: coastal zone, middle zone and inland zone.

373 Closest to the sea, the trees of the coastal zone must deal with the heavy salty water of this zone. These trees typically have thin, pencil-like roots sticking out. These aerial roots are efficient at filtering salt and oxygen absorption. These hardy trees stay rooted, and their roots are high enough to weather high tides.

OCEAN ECOSYSTEMS

374
The trees in the middle zone usually have prop roots. These long branching roots help the trees to stand upright in the soft soil and absorb oxygen. They usually grow in large numbers. Trees in the inland zone must deal with high salinity because the process of evaporation often leaves heavy deposits of salt.

375
The mangrove forests are one of the most important ecological systems in the world. These forests are teeming with life, from the roots to the treetops. Some species spend their entire life in these forests, while other come here for breeding and nourishment. As an intertidal zone, it is a crucial habitat for many species.

376
The mangroves serve many purposes for their inhabitants. For many, it acts as a nursery and rookery. A number of marine species, from crabs to large fishes, lay their eggs here. The juvenile fishes often stay on for nourishment before moving on to the ocean. It is also home to many marine birds, who use it for breeding and shelter.

A thorny oyster grows among colourful prop roots in a mangrove forest in Raja Ampat, Indonesia.

MANGROVE FORESTS

377 There are several animals, birds and invertebrates who come to the mangroves for food. At high tide we can find a large number of marine predators—from crocodile to fish—that come here chasing or looking for their prey. The mangroves are known for their large predators including the estuarine crocs and the Bengal tiger.

378 One of the most important inhabitants of the mangroves are crabs. They are considered a keynote species here. This means that their presence is critical for other species to live here. The crabs feed on the mangrove leaves, reducing leaf litter. Their burrows keep the soil aerated. They also act as a food source for predator species.

379 The mangroves are home to a bacteria that is critical for the marine ecosystem. The bacteria break down the dead leaves and branches of the trees. In the process, they release nutrients which then fall into the sea. This detritus provides energy and food to marine species, forming the base of the marine food chain.

OCEAN ECOSYSTEMS

380 **We cannot underestimate the importance of mangroves as an ecological system.** They provide the necessary shelter and breeding ground for many species. Their ability to nurture and provide food is critically important for our marine species. Apart from that, they are vital for maintaining the coastal populations and environmental balance.

381 **The fish and crustaceans living among the mangroves are an important source of food for local human communities.** In fact, local communities are now working actively to save these natural fisheries. Other products generated from mangroves like honey and oil, corks, soaps and dyes also have wide commercial use.

382 **As an interface between the sea and land, mangroves are also environmentally very important.** They buffer the coastal regions against violent storms. They hold together the loose soil at the coasts, stopping it from washing away. But more importantly, mangroves can increase the landmass. By planting these trees at the edges of the coast, some coastal communities have reclaimed land!

MANGROVE FORESTS

383 **Mangroves are also very useful in dealing with climate change.** Trees are critical in fighting climate change because they store carbon in their biomass, reducing the effect of increasing carbon dioxide emissions in the atmosphere. Mangroves are particularly good at this, storing almost five times the amount absorbed by a rainforest of an equal area.

384 **Another important wetland ecosystem is the salt marsh.** We can find them in the intertidal zone, which is frequently flooded with salty or brackish water. They are called the mangroves of the temperate and Arctic regions. But unlike mangroves, salt marshes are a little poor in vegetation, containing mostly shrubs.

385 **Salt marshes are tenacious, and are found in a number of coastal regions, especially estuaries.** They are also found on open coasts, lagoons, deltas, and hardier ground-like cliffs and rocky shores. With their wide expanse and short shrubs, salt marshes are also ideal for human habitation. For example, the Mississippi Delta in the USA has an extensive salt marsh network.

OCEAN ECOSYSTEMS

386 Like the mangroves, plants in the salt marsh must adapt to salinity and low oxygen conditions. They must also adapt to bouts of flooding and exposure. The saltwater plant adaption is, in fact, quite similar to that of a mangrove. For instance, they have a similar method of filtering out salt intake by using negative pressure.

387 The salt marsh plants have succulent leaves and stems that are useful to store water. Most species can store salt in their tissue, while some have special glands at the base of their leaves to process the salt content. They also have special short-lived roots that help in absorption of nutrients and oxygen uptake.

388 Salt marshes show a clear pattern of zones that is decided by its pattern of flooding. These zones are: the low marsh, high marsh, planes, pools and upland border. The zones are reflected in the plant species that grow there, since they must adapt to the water conditions in their zone.

MANGROVE FORESTS

389 **The low marsh is found at the seaward edge along the shoreline.** This is usually a narrow intertidal band of land. It sees alternating periods of flooding (during high tide) and exposure (during low tide). The salinity remains constant. Plant species here are well-adapted to high salinity, regular flooding and exposure, like smooth cordgrass.

390 **The high marsh lies between the low marsh and upland border.** Flooding here is less frequent, only seen in case of unusually high tides. Diversity in plant species is low, limited to grasses and rushes. The high marsh can also have pools of water. These dry up during summer, increasing the salinity. Hence, plant species must be able to tolerate high salinity.

Border of a salt marsh

391 **After this comes the border of the salt marsh.** This area is rarely flooded. As a result, it has wider plant diversity, including herbs, shrubs, grasses and even trees. In some cases, we may even have an influx of freshwater in the marsh, forming an Oligohaline Marsh. Here, we find a mix of freshwater and marine plants.

OCEAN ECOSYSTEMS

392 Some important inhabitants of the salt marsh are the numerous algae species that live here. Although their function is similar to that of plants, their growth and decomposition is quicker, providing a quick and more efficient source of nutrition to the marine species that live here. They are often the base of the marsh food chain.

393 The salt marshes are thriving ecosystems. They support a number of fish, birds and mammals. The inhabitants of the marsh add to its health. For example, herbivores break down the plant leaves, stems and shoots, and provide a food source to the predators. Further, creatures like crabs create burrows that help aerate the oxygen-poor soil.

A diamondback terrapin, found in salt marshes.

394 As an intertidal ecosystem, salt marshes are critical sheltering points for their inhabitants. From invertebrates to birds, many of them come here for shelter and breeding. For many birds, salt marshes are also their wintering grounds. Salt marshes are also used by humans for agriculture, salt production and as grounds for further urban development.

A great white egret standing in water in a marsh.

Seagrass Bed

395 **Another important marine ecosystem is the seagrass bed.** Except for Antarctica, almost all coastal regions have seagrass beds. These highly productive ecosystems provide support and shelter to a number of marine species. Found underwater in marine or brackish water, some seagrass beds are so densely packed that you can actually see them from space!

396 **Seagrass may look like grass, but it is actually a plant!** It has roots, stems and leaves. It produces flowers and seeds. It also uses photosynthesis to produce food and energy. Seagrasses are quite ancient, dating back to 100 million years ago. There are roughly 72 different species of seagrass.

397 **Seagrass has several special adaptions that helps it to cope with its underwater habitat.** These plants have little air pockets that keep them buoyant. Instead of stomata (tiny opening for exchange of gas and water), they have a thin layer on the leaves for direct diffusion of nutrients. The roots act as an anchor, and a place of storage for nutrients.

A queen conch (stromus gigas) lies on a shallow seagrass bed in the Caribbean Sea.

OCEAN ECOSYSTEMS

Octopus and amphora hiding in the middle of a seagrass bed.

398
Seagrass ecosystems are extremely important and powerful. These plants are known as ecosystem engineers because they can change their own environment, creating suitable conditions for other organisms to grow. These biodiversity hotspots form the habitat for hundreds of small organisms, which in turn attract bigger predators. One estimate suggests that the population of just an acre of seagrass has 40,000 fish and 50 million invertebrates!

399
Did you know that seagrasses are also called the 'lungs of the sea'? They have the ability to produce oxygen through photosynthesis. They can also absorb nutrients through their leaves, reducing runoff from land. In low nutrient areas, they help in releasing nutrients to the surroundings. The roots are also important in trapping soil and sediments, preventing it from washing away.

400
Marine ecosystems play a vital role in our environment. They not only provide shelter, breeding and hunting grounds, they are also vital in keeping the environmental balance of this planet. They help in fighting climate change, protecting shorelines, nurturing several important species and providing livelihood to millions of people. Their conservation and protection is critical for our planet.

UNDERSEA GEOLOGY

Seamounts, Underwater Earthquakes and Volcanoes

401 **What lies beneath our oceans?** At the very bottom of the ocean is the ocean floor and just like land, disturbances on the ocean floor can have far-reaching effects. These changes affect marine habitats, weather pattens and over the years, it can change the very surface of earth. So, let's look a little deeper into our oceans and walk its floor!

402 We have to be careful while walking on the ocean floor. You may think that the ocean floor is an even, smooth basin on which the ocean water flows, but the truth is that it can get very rocky! There are hills, mountains, valleys and treacherous pits. There are even volcanoes and earthquakes underwater!

403 If you are wondering why the ocean floor looks so rocky, then blame the plate tectonics! The earth's surface is made up of parts called 'plates'. All the continents and oceans are located on these plates. Underneath this, lies partially melted rock. But these plates are almost constantly moving. It is this movement that gives the ocean floor its ridges, mountains and valleys.

UNDERSEA GEOLOGY

404 If the earth's plates are always moving, why don't we feel it? It's because this movement is so slow that we do not even notice it. But if you've felt an earthquake, then you know how it feels! The theory that the earth is divided into plates that are constantly moving is known as 'plate tectonics'.

405 **The movement of plates in relation to each other decides the nature of their boundaries.** There are three types of boundaries: transform, divergent and convergent. In transform boundaries, a plate slides or grazes along another one. In divergent boundaries, two plates move away from each other. In convergent boundaries, two plates move towards each other.

THREE TYPES OF PLATE BOUNDARY

Divergent plate boundary

Transform plate boundary

Convergent plate boundary

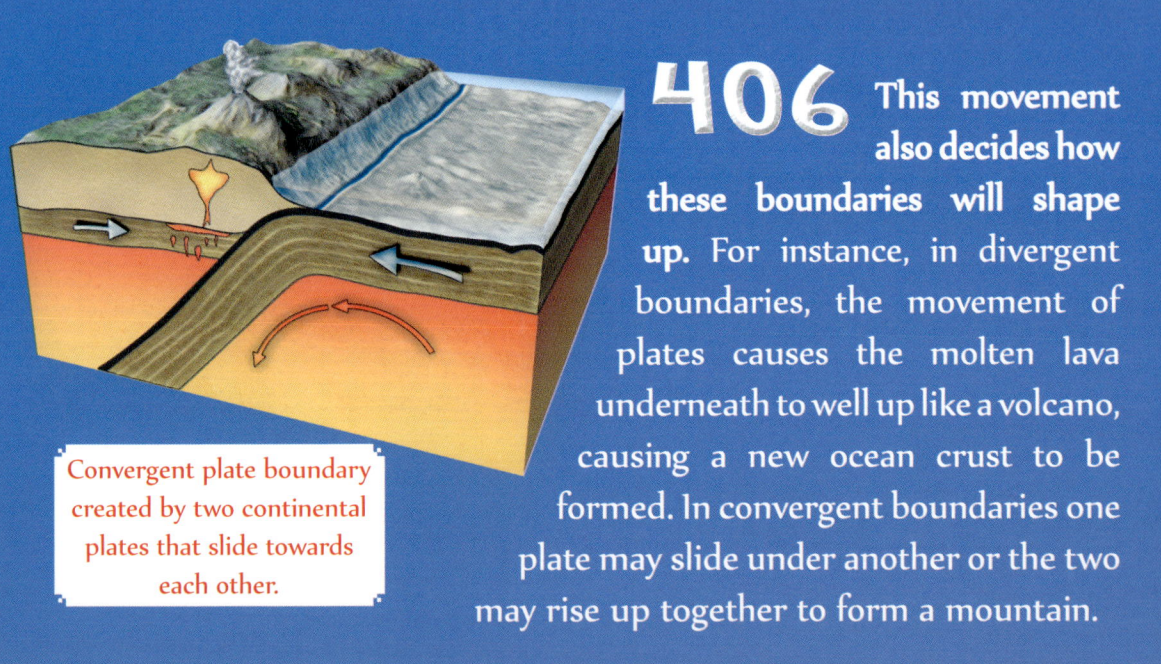

406 **This movement also decides how these boundaries will shape up.** For instance, in divergent boundaries, the movement of plates causes the molten lava underneath to well up like a volcano, causing a new ocean crust to be formed. In convergent boundaries one plate may slide under another or the two may rise up together to form a mountain.

Convergent plate boundary created by two continental plates that slide towards each other.

SEAMOUNTS, UNDERWATER EARTHQUAKES AND VOLCANOES

407 **Sometimes, there appears a deep fissure in the ocean bed.** This is an ocean trench. A trench is a deep narrow depression in the floor, like a canyon. These trenches are the deepest parts of the earth. Trenches occur at convergent plate boundaries when one plate goes under the other one.

408 **Can you name the deepest part of the ocean?** It is a spot known as the Challenger Deep in the Mariana Trench, located in the Western Pacific Ocean. It is so deep that even if you dropped the Mount Everest down this spot, you would still have more than a mile of ocean above its peak!

409 **Try to answer this question: which is the tallest mountain on earth?** No, it's not Mount Everest! The tallest mountain on earth, from base to summit, is Mauna Kea in Hawaii. But if you wanted to climb it from the base, you would have to drop down 6,000 metres below the sea! Mount Kea is a seamount, one of the massive underwater mountains, of which only the peak is visible above water level.

Mauna Kea Summit on Big Island of Hawaii

UNDERSEA GEOLOGY

410 Did you know, that you may see a number of towering mountains, known as seamounts, if you were to walk the ocean floor? They make navigation a little tough, but they are full of life. From their base in the deep ocean floor, to their summit that reaches above water, the seamounts are full of biodiversity, including corals that thrive in cold water conditions.

411 **Seamounts are present in all the oceans.** So far, we have mapped only about 10,000 of these. Some oceanographers believe that there are millions of seamounts, more than the mountains on land! Seamounts are usually found near plate boundaries where the lava underneath has welled up to create new crust.

412 **The minimum height of a seamount is 1,000 metres.** But many of these seamounts can reach great heights. The Great Meteor Tablemount, located in the North-East Atlantic, is over 4,000 metres from base to tip. It is surrounded by smaller seamounts. Scientists believe that this formation was once located just below the North American continent.

SEAMOUNTS, UNDERWATER EARTHQUAKES AND VOLCANOES

413 **Seamounts are usually found in clusters.** Since they develop because of plate tectonics, the cluster is found along the lines of plate boundaries. The cluster is typically linear which means they form along a line and not as a random grouping. Almost all seamounts develop as a result of volcanic activity when the inner mantle pushes up and creates these underwater mountains.

414 **A seamount with a flat top is called a guyot or a tabletop.** They are found mostly in the Pacific Ocean, at a depth of 1,000 to 2,000 metres below the ocean surface. These tend to be at least 914 metres tall. There are other elevations — shorter than these — which are called oceanic plateaus.

415 **Do you know why a guyot has a flat surface, whereas seamounts have a peak?** One theory suggests that it is because of the original size of a guyot which initially rose above the sea surface. Over time, wave erosion cut away the top, making it flat. Eventually, the guyots sink furthur because of the gradual movement and slow sinking of the ocean floor.

UNDERSEA GEOLOGY

A sea turtle near volcanic rocks in the ocean near the Galapagos Islands.

416 Did you know that 80 per cent of volcanic eruptions on the planet take place in the ocean? Scientists estimate that there are millions of such volcanoes scattered across the floor of the oceans. These volcanoes are also some of the most productive regions in the world. On the deep ocean floor, the gases produced by the volcanic eruptions provide nutrients for life to flourish.

417 Have you ever wondered how a volcano can erupt in the ocean when we cannot even light a matchstick underwater? Actually, underwater volcanoes are not like the usual volcanoes that we see on land. The lava cools down and then solidifies quickly, taking on an almost pillowy-shaped flow. The temperature, pressure and the chemical composition of the water changes around a volcanic site.

418 These submarine volcanoes are usually located along the plate boundaries. The magma from under the ground wells up and settles around the point of eruption. With time, it piles up and can even rise above the surface, creating volcanic islands like Hawaii. This is how a seamount is formed. Most of these volcanoes are found around the mid-ocean ridge.

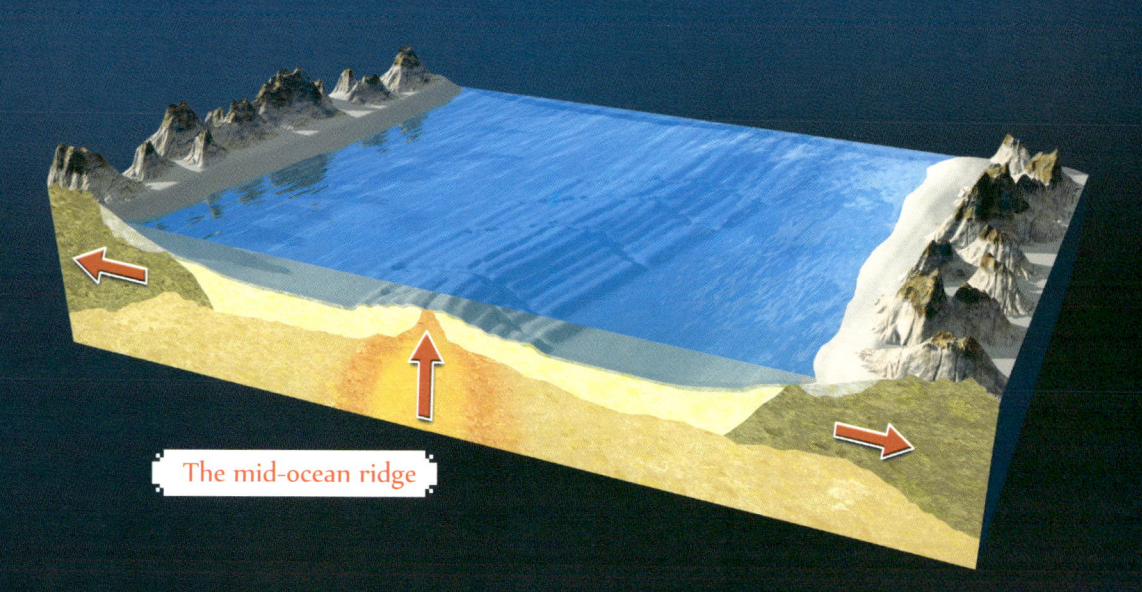

SEAMOUNTS, UNDERWATER EARTHQUAKES AND VOLCANOES

The mid-ocean ridge

419 Did you know that the longest mountain chain actually lies beneath the ocean? This is the mid-ocean ridge. It is composed of a number of underwater ridges, that are interconnected. The 65,000 kilometres long chain goes around the earth.

420 **The mid-ocean ridge is present in all the oceans.** It occurs around a line of divergent plate boundaries. As the plates move away from each other, molten rock from underneath wells up. Some of this molten rock produces impressive volcanoes. At this point, you will see a stream of lava, underwater volcanoes and hydrothermal vents.

421 **If there is a chain of mountains and volcanoes around the globe, why don't we notice it?** Well, sometimes we do. In 1783, a part of the ridge which appears above the sea in Iceland erupted in a massive volcanic eruption. But most of the ridge is at least 2,000 metres deep. In fact, our most accurate information about these phenomena has been collected by scientists in just the last 10 years or so!

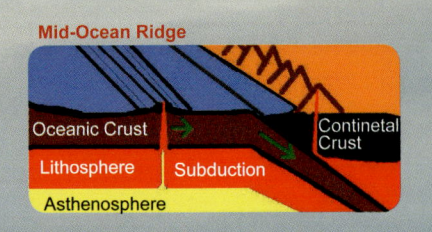

UNDERSEA GEOLOGY

422 Mountains are not actually the most interesting part of the mid-ocean ridge. Scientists realised that this constant flow of lava had another far-reaching consequence—the expansion of our seafloor, or seafloor spreading. Scientists say that the constant underwater eruptions keep adding layers of lava, creating new ocean crust constantly. This lava flows away from the ridge, thus 'spreading' the seafloor!

423 At the divergent boundary of the mid-ocean ridge, the tectonic plates are slowly moving away from each other. This is a very slow movement, caused by the gradual churning of the earth's mantle. The hot matter of the mantle moves up and makes the crust less dense, and almost flexible. As the lighter plate moves up, it eventually results in formation of undersea mountains.

424 As the mantle pushes up, the crust eventually cracks. The hot magma wells up through the cracks and flows out. Under the cold water and intense pressure conditions, the magma cools rapidly and hardens into basalt and igneous rock. This is a slow and continuous process, where the magma pours out constantly creating new crust.

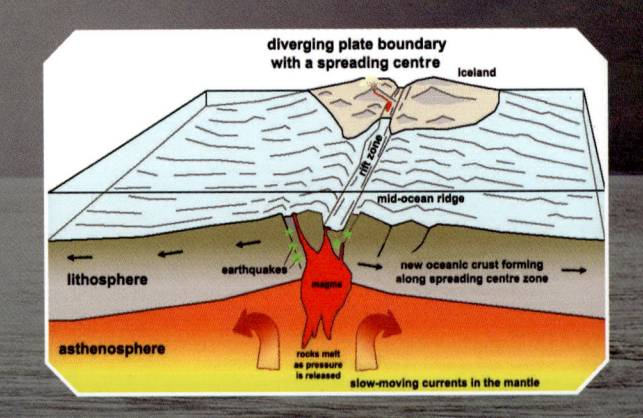

SEAMOUNTS, UNDERWATER EARTHQUAKES AND VOLCANOES

425 **The rate of separation is not constant at all points on the ridge, and it shows in the surrounding surface.** Where the separation is slow, we find tall tapered hills and seamounts. On rapidly spreading ridges, the slope is gentler. The centre of the ridge is the actual site of the separation. This is where the newest crust is found!

426 **As the crust moves away from the ridge, it cools down, becoming thicker and denser.** Eventually it meets another plate boundary. What happens at these meeting points often decides the area's geographical structure. This interaction is also the reason behind the different ocean floor features and phenomenons like volcanoes and earthquakes.

427 **In some cases, the oceanic plate crashes into the continental plate (a tectonic plate that is under a continent), resulting in volcanoes and earthquakes.** In other cases, the plate may transition to the ocean floor and then to the continental crust. The first is known as an active plate margin, while the second is a passive plate margin.

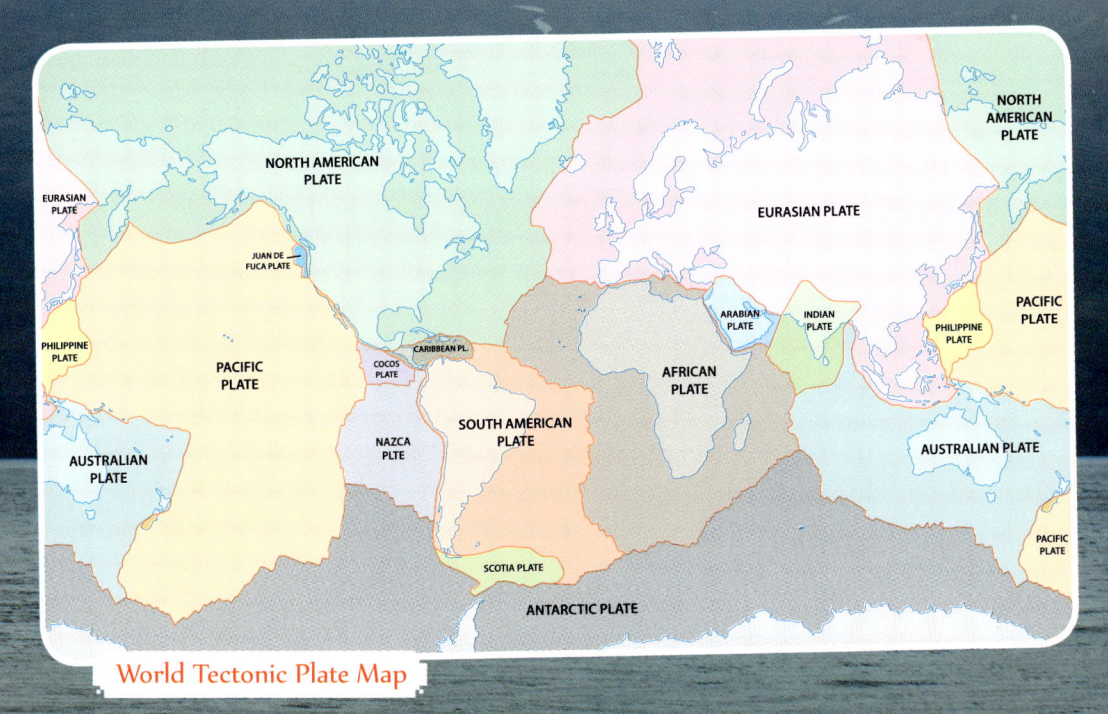

World Tectonic Plate Map

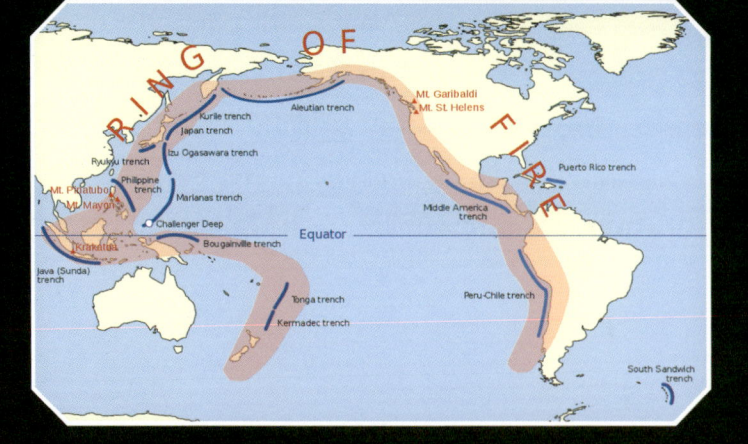

428 **Now that you know most volcanoes are underwater, can you name the longest chain of volcanoes?** The answer is the Ring of Fire which lies on the fringes of the Pacific Ocean. Apart from explosive volcanoes, this is a place where you will find the maximum number of earthquakes!

429 **The Ring of Fire is roughly a horseshoe-shaped ring that stretches over 40,000 kilometres and accounts for close to 90 per cent of the world's earthquakes and over 75 per cent of its volcanoes (active and dormant).** Not just in numbers, these volcanoes and earthquakes are also some of the most massive in scale in recent history.

430 **The Ring of Fire is also the perfect example of an active plate margin.** At this point, the oceanic plates crash into the continental plates. At the boundary, the denser oceanic plate is shoved downwards. The friction causes the oceanic plate to heat up and become molten. This is the hot magma which breaks through the upper continental plate in the form of a volcano.

SEAMOUNTS, UNDERWATER EARTHQUAKES AND VOLCANOES

431 **The Ring of Fire has an almost continuous stretch of deep trenches where the plate bends down before going under.** Some of the earth's most powerful earthquakes occur here. This happens when two plates scrape against each other. This makes the region one of the most volatile on the planet, with earthquakes and volcanic mountains in the surrounding area.

432 **The movement of tectonic plates can often cause havoc and devastation.** The most common example that we can see are earthquakes. Whether they occur close to the land or in the deep sea, an underwater earthquake can have a devastating impact if it is strong enough. Apart from shaking the earth's surface in a quake, it can also release the pent-up gases from beneath the crust.

433 **Minor stress lines or faults can appear because of plate interactions and are uneventful.** But sometimes these interactions are a little jarring. For instance, when one plate goes under another or when two plates scrape past each other violently. In both cases there is a sudden violent movement which we know as an earthquake.

Earth's fault lines between tectonic plates

UNDERSEA GEOLOGY

434 **An underwater earthquake can have a devastating effect by changing the surface of the ocean floor.** An earthquake where a tectonic plate rises or falls suddenly, causes the water above to swell as a higher than usual wave. This wave rolls ahead in the ocean and becomes a giant wave. This is known as a tsunami.

435 **When a tsunami starts in the deep ocean, the height of the wave is only around a foot.** But it grows and moves with tremendous speed. It races across the ocean at almost 500 miles an hour. As the waves come closer to the shoreline, their speed decreases, but their height and energy is now massive.

436 **When the tsunami reaches land, its trough (low point of the wave) hits the shore first.** So tremendous is its energy that it can pull away the ocean water near the shore, exposing the harbour. Immediately after that, the massive wave hits the shore. But remember, the tsunami comes in waves, and the really destructive waves actually follow a little later!

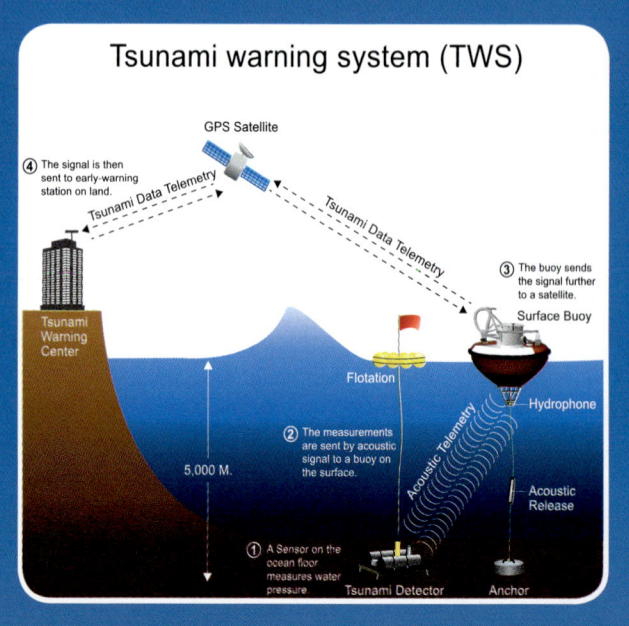

Tsunami warning system (TWS)

① A Sensor on the ocean floor measures water pressure.
② The measurements are sent by acoustic signal to a buoy on the surface.
③ The buoy sends the signal further to a satellite.
④ The signal is then sent to early-warning station on land.

437 **The spreading seafloor has resulted in another profound impact which takes place so slowly that we hardly notice it.** As the seafloor 'spreads' and the tectonic plates push away from the mid-ocean ridge, it causes a ripple effect. Eventually, this can move whole continents. This movement is called the continental drift.

SEAMOUNTS, UNDERWATER EARTHQUAKES AND VOLCANOES

438 **Scientists believe that the different continents on earth have broken apart and joined many times.** They believe the landmasses can join into one big supercontinent. The last supercontinent was Pangea, around 300 million years ago. Plate tectonics and seafloor spreading pushes the continental plates, moving around the continents over a period of time.

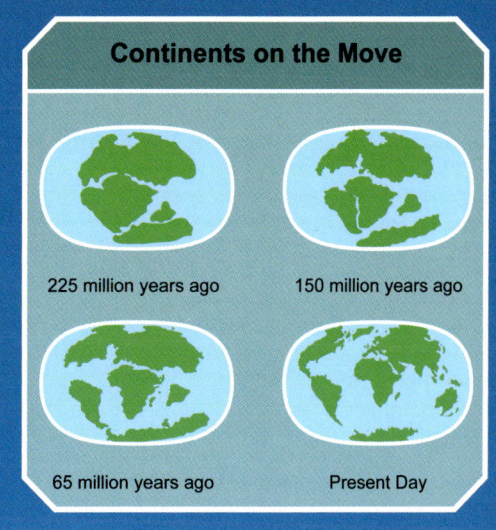

Continents on the Move

225 million years ago | 150 million years ago
65 million years ago | Present Day

Continental drift on earth, showing Pangaea, Laurasia, Gondwana and modern continents.

439 **If you look at the world map, you will get clear clues of the continental drift.** The east coast of South America seems perfectly aligned to the west coast of Africa! Often, fossils of plants and animals at one continent are actually natives of another continent! These findings indicate that these continents were once very close together.

440 **Thus, the ocean floor is an uneven collection of deep trenches, mountains, fissures, volcanoes and even earthquakes.** The ocean and its floor is clearly a very busy place, which is always changing, moving and renewing itself. In the process, it changes our continents and shapes our world!

EXPLORING THE OCEAN

Incredible Technology

441 **Although oceans cover more than 70 per cent of our planet and provide a home to millions of living beings, we still know very little about them.** The main reason for this is the inaccessibility of studying the deep ocean. Hence, most of our knowledge is limited to shallow waters that are easily reached.

442 **Understanding and studying the ocean has become increasingly important because the ocean is a rich source of food, energy and other natural resources.** It also helps us to understand the weather and climate patterns influenced by oceans. Finally, the study of ocean floor tells us about crust movements, earthquakes and tsunamis.

Gas production platform on the sea

INCREDIBLE TECHNOLOGY

443 The study of the underwater ocean or ocean floor is known as 'bathymetry'. It comes from the Greek words- bathus and metron, which means 'deep' and 'measure'. Today, the study focuses on underwater navigation, exploration of the deep ocean and mapping of the oceans.

444 What makes the study of the deep ocean so difficult? This is mainly because the conditions in deep oceans are extremely hostile for us. It is frigidly cold and pitch-dark. To top it all, the pressure under all that water is so immense that we would die before we reach anywhere close to the deep ocean floor.

445 The inhospitable conditions in the deep ocean have forced us to come up with innovative methods. The only way we can explore the deep ocean is through technology, like using sonar or submersibles to reach the ocean floor. Explorers have also developed specialised diving equipment that allows them to dive to great depths.

EXPLORING THE OCEAN

446 **An essential part of the ocean exploration is the vessel that is used.** It is a specially equipped shipping vessel that has state of the art electronics and equipment for navigation and communication like sonar systems. The vessel is also used as a laboratory for gathering and studying oceanic data as well as housing equipment that is essential for studying the ocean.

447 **The only way to explore the deepest portions of our oceans is through submersible vessels.** These specially designed vessels can withstand extremes in temperature and pressure. A submersible can dive down to great depths and allows us to reach deep ocean trenches. This is how explorers discovered life in these extremely hostile conditions.

448 **Submersibles are not just useful for exploration, they are also used to collect samples from the deep sea.** Researchers use manned or unmanned submersibles to collect living and non-living samples like microbes. They are also used to take photographs and videos that give us a rare glimpse into the very depths of the ocean where even light cannot reach.

INCREDIBLE TECHNOLOGY

449 Today, we also have very specialised equipment to carry out a detailed and systematic study of the ocean. These include satellites, special recording equipment that detect and record our noisy oceans, nets that can collect specimens, and other equipment that can help us study currents. Equipment like CTDs (which stands for 'conductivity, temperature and depth'), help us to correctly gauge the physical and chemical properties of ocean water.

450 One of the oldest and most commonly used technology is sonar. Here, we use sound waves to study the ocean floor. When sound waves bounce off the floor, they create an echo. Since we already know the speed of sound in ocean water, the time it takes for us to hear an echo tells us the true depth of the ocean.

451 Although the ocean is such a vast space, its exploration is conducted in a precise, scientific manner. Over the years, it has given us a clearer picture of the ocean and the ocean floor. It has helped us determine the effect of the ocean on earth's climate and how the oceans are changing in relation to changes in the climate.

EXPLORING THE OCEAN

452 Deep sea exploration has another vital function—mapping our oceans. Although most people think of the ocean as a single flat surface, it actually has an amazing topography. We have already learnt about the longest range of mountains, deep trenches, canyons, cliffs and vast areas of vegetation—all underwater!

453 Did you know that we still have no detailed maps of the ocean floor? Although we have extremely accurate maps of all continents, only about five per cent of the ocean floor is mapped in detail! Considering that most of the earth is covered in oceans, this also means that most of the earth is not mapped despite technological advancement!

454 Why are there no detailed maps of the ocean floor? The reasons that make deep sea exploration so difficult are also the causes for the difficulty in mapping the ocean. Although we have developed some idea of the ocean floor, in reality most of this is based on calculations and estimates. Most of the time we only have blurry outlines, without any details.

INCREDIBLE TECHNOLOGY

455 **The parts of the ocean floor that are well-mapped are usually confined to coastal regions and continental shelves.** Because these are easy to reach and explore, oceanographers have developed fairly accurate maps of these regions. Other areas include ocean floor under major shipping lines. These areas were mapped in some detail because of their commercial importance.

456 **Interestingly, many of our maps of the deep ocean floor actually come from outer space!** Satellites have plotted and mapped much of the unexplored ocean floor. But this is highly blurry. Although it may give us some idea of the topography, it fails to provide us with valuable details, such as the depth of canyons and trenches.

Central America Satellite Space Map Composition

457 **The most accurate tools for mapping the ocean floor use sonar technology.** Today, we have highly developed sonars that can produce very accurate results. Multiple sound waves are sent and received by vessels built for this purpose. This information is fed into specially designed computers with programs that can generate detailed maps.

EXPLORING THE OCEAN

458 Sonar methods have given us a remarkable means of studying and mapping the oceans. Oceanographers not only use multiple sonars for gathering data, they also often use different frequencies. A standard frequency tells them about the depth of the ocean floor, while a lower frequency can tell them about the different sediments that lie beneath!

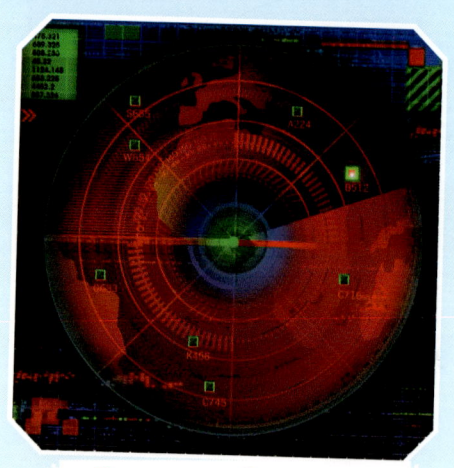

Different sonar frequencies are used for different parameters.

459 Both satellite and sonar methods have their own pros and cons. Unlike the satellite method, sonars can map only a limited area at a time. However, they give us a far more accurate result. Most detailed ocean maps use both—satellite images for more inaccessible regions, and sonar images whenever these are available.

460 If ocean mapping is so difficult, why are we still so interested in trying to do so? The reasons are many. The first is, of course, because the ocean forms a vast portion of the earth. We know more about the moon than we know about the ocean floor! The other reason is its unique topography which affects the entire planet in many ways.

OCEAN LEGENDS

Mythology

461 Humans have such a long association with oceans, it is not surprising that it has played a role in human mythology as well. Interestingly, gods of the ocean are present in almost all mythologies, across the world. For the ancient man, these gods helped them to deal with the ocean that they did not fully understand.

462 Poseidon was the ancient Olympian god of the oceans and king of the sea gods. He was also the god of rivers, floods, storms, droughts, earthquakes and strangely, horses. According to mythology, he became the god of seas after he helped his brothers imprison the old gods. He is often depicted as a mature man with a beard and a trident.

Poseidon, Olympian god of the oceans

463 The ancient Roman counterpart of Poseidon was Neptune. In fact, the Roman god shares several similarities with the ancient Greek god. He is the god of the sea, holder of a trident and also the creator of horses. Some of his depictions were also similar, with long hair, beard, trident and chariot.

OCEAN LEGENDS

464 **In Haiti, the loa (god's intermediary) Agwé rules over the sea, aquatic plants and fish.** He is also the patron loa of sailors and fishermen. If pleased, Agwé can bless you with riches that are lost at sea. Offerings to Agwe are dropped off board or left on rafts. There are strict rules, which if ignored will anger Agwe.

465 **As the son of Poseidon, the Greek god, Triton, was believed to be the messenger of the sea.** Although, like his father he too carries a trident, his conch is really his most important weapon. He uses it to calm or raise waves. Triton is represented as a merman, with the upper body of a man and the tail of a fish.

Greek god Triton, messenger of the sea

466 **The Dragon Kings of the Four Seas were water and weather gods in the Chinese folk religion.** The four dragon kings represent the seas in the four cardinal directions. It was believed that these powerful gods could not only make it rain, they could also take any number of forms. They were a symbol of masculine power, strength and good luck.

A carving at a Dragon King temple.

MYTHOLOGY

467 **Did you know that the Chinese water god, Gonggong, was frequently also seen as a sea monster?** In many stories, he is sent into exile, or killed. The stories also blame him for a host of calamities, especially floods. But he does seem to have great power. Upset over a defeat, he once threw a tantrum, knocking the earth off its axis!

468 **In ancient Mesopotamian religion, Tiamat was the goddess of the ocean.** Through her marriage with Abzu (god of freshwater), she gave birth to younger gods. But according to a legend, she was also the bringer of great destruction, waging war on her children and unleashing chaos. According to these myths, it was from her slain body that the entire physical world emerged!

469 **The god of the undersea world in the northwestern Native American Pacific mythology was the fearsome Kumugwe.** Not only did he live in a house under the sea full of riches, his house was quite literally made of living sea lions and his world guarded by an octopus! Apart from his power over the seas and its riches, Kumugwe could see the future!

470 **The god from whose name we get the word 'ocean' is the Greek and Roman god Oceanus.** In the ancient Greek mythology, Oceanus was the divine impersonation of the sea, which they saw as a huge river circling the flat earth. He was also the god of all freshwater- from rivers to lakes.

Sculpture of Oceanus in the Trevi Fountain of Rome, Italy.

Legends of the Ocean

471 For sailors who often had to sail across its turbulent waters, the ocean was dangerous, mysterious and sometimes, the land of strange and terrifying creatures. Human imagination would give colour to the unknown and this is why we have the legends of the ocean. Some of these are based on actual creatures and some seem absolute fantasy.

472 Off the coasts of Greenland and Norway, was believed to be the home of the legendary giant kraken. Although, initial accounts described it as something that resembled a crab with some whale-like characteristics, many people now believe that it was probably a description of a giant squid. First described by Erik Pontoppidan in 1752, the Kraken has since become a legendary sea monster.

The legendary kraken

LEGENDS OF THE OCEAN

473 **The Lady of the Lake, an aquatic spirit and ruler of the mythical Avalon of Arthurian legend is known by many names—Nimue, Elaine, Viviane, Vivien, and more.** Some stories see these ladies as being different, and succeeding one another. She is most famous for handing over the sword Excalibur, to King Arthur and entrapping Merlin. She is also said to have brought up Sir Lancelot after his father's death.

474 **A very famous legend of the modern age is Moby Dick, the whale from the novel of the same title.** Published in 1851, the novel was written by the American novelist Herman Melville. Although *Moby Dick* was entirely fictional, it was based on an actual incident where a sperm whale had attacked a whaling ship.

Herman Melville

475 **Nessie or the Loch Ness Monster is an inhabitant of the Loch Ness (a lake) in Scotland.** It is believed to have a long neck and one or two humps on its back. Some people think that it is a dinosaur. However, scientists point out that the lake is too small for a dinosaur! Whether it exists or not, Nessie is an enduring figure in Scottish folklore.

An illustration of the Loch Ness Monster.

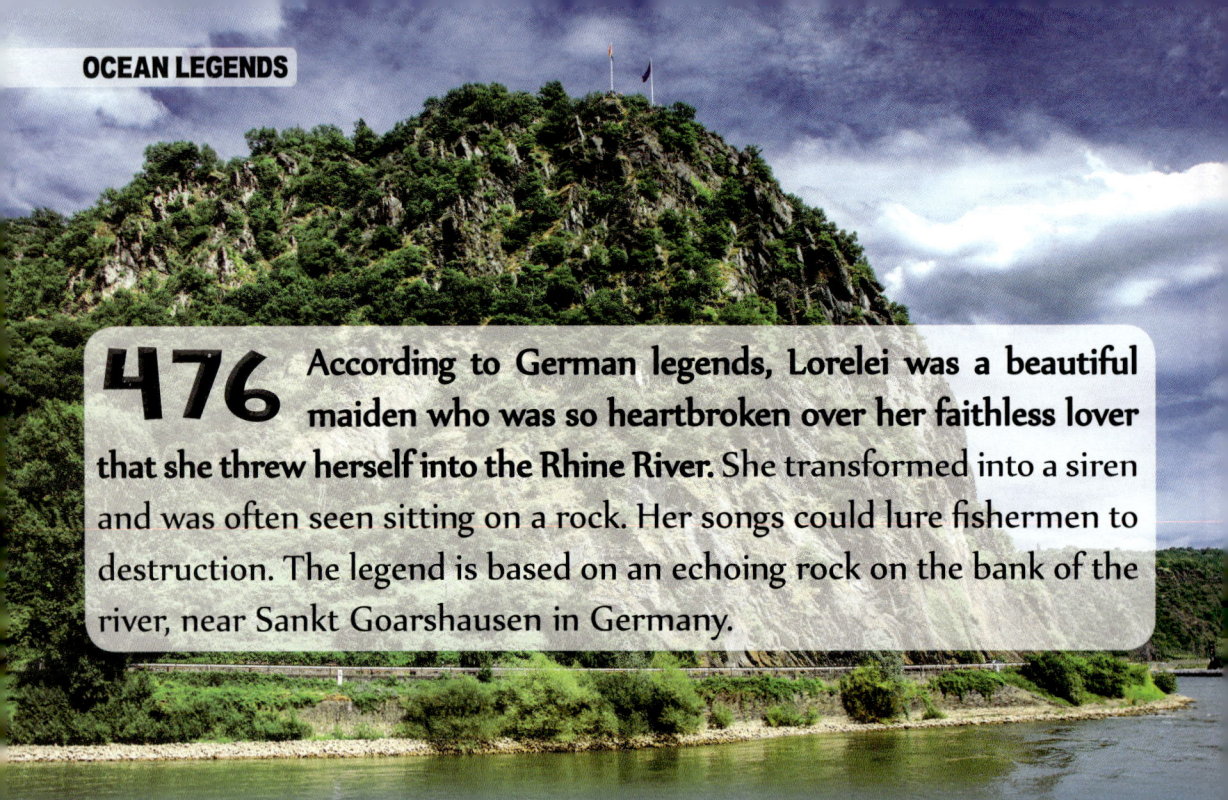

OCEAN LEGENDS

476 According to German legends, Lorelei was a beautiful maiden who was so heartbroken over her faithless lover that she threw herself into the Rhine River. She transformed into a siren and was often seen sitting on a rock. Her songs could lure fishermen to destruction. The legend is based on an echoing rock on the bank of the river, near Sankt Goarshausen in Germany.

477 Kappas are demons or imps in traditional Japanese folklore. The word comes from Japanese words for 'river' and 'child'. The legend of Kappas seems to vary slightly from one region to another. These legends are used to warn people about the dangers of rivers. Some people think they are based on river otters, while others say it is based on the Japanese giant salamander.

A statue of Kappa

478 Perhaps one of the most enduring and fascinating ocean legends is that of the Mer people. Mermaids appear in many coastal folklores from around the world—from Africa to Asia. Some stories see them as loving, gentle and mysterious, while some associate them with shipwrecks and storms. Their male counterparts are the mermen. The menfolk, according to some legends, live in the deep ocean!

The Little Mermaid statue in Copenhagen, Denmark.

LEGENDS OF THE OCEAN

479 **The Nereids were nymphs, daughters of sea god Nereus in Greek mythology.** They represented the rich bounty of the ocean. These friendly goddesses were protectors of fishermen and sailors, coming to the aid of anyone who needed them. They were seen as beautiful creatures, playing with sea creatures like dolphins.

The Hispalis fountain in Serville, Spain, featuring Nereids.

480 **Unlike the Nereids, the sirens of Greek mythology were far more dangerous.** They lived in the sea and lured sailors with their enchanting call or music, leading them to shipwrecks on the rocky shores. They appear in many Greek and Roman legends and sport many horrible qualities, including cannibalism! The phrase 'siren song' originates from their legend.

481 **Almost as old as the story of commercial shipping, is the legend of pirates.** Unlike the fantasy characters of myths and stories, these were men of flesh and blood who could strike terror in the heart of every ship's captain. Many of their stories are shrouded in myths and legends. Piracy on seas still remains a major concern today.

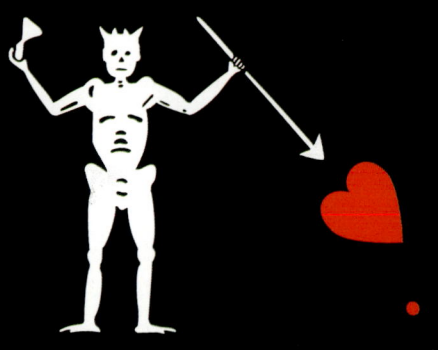

Notorious pirate Blackbeard's pirate flag.

482 **Most pirates of the legend were British brigands of the 1500s–1700s.** They had found a shortcut to wealth—looting ships coming from the rich colonies of Asia or the Americas, on their way home to England or Spain. However, this was not as common as it may seem, because it took a lot to maintain a crew big enough to take over another ship.

PIRATES AND FAMOUS LOOT

483 **One of the most fearsome legends is that of Blackbeard (1680–1718).** He carefully cultivated his fearsome appearance to establish his reputation. Born as Edward Teach in Britain, his area of operation was the eastern coast of North America and around the West Indies. He once held an entire crew ransom, until the port town of Charleston, South Carolina had to pay up to release them!

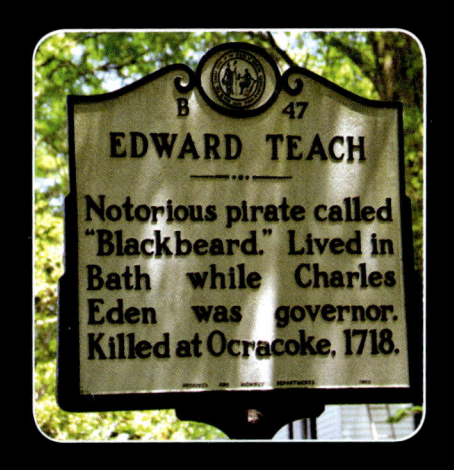

484 **If you thought all pirates led disgraced lives and died in battles, meet the pirate Captain Morgan, who later became Sir Henry Morgan!** He raided and looted a number of Spanish ships, amassing considerable wealth. He was appointed as the Lieutenant Governor of Jamaica from where he continued his exploits, eventually becoming a wealthy landowner.

485 **Captain Morgan was an exception to the pirate norm.** Most pirates, like Thomas Tew, died young in bloody battles or they were captured and executed. Tew, a 17th century English pirate, led two major voyages, dying in a battle on his second voyage. He is mainly credited with the invention of the 'pirate round', which was a piracy route. Even in his limited time on sea, he amassed great wealth, which would today amount to about $103 million!

Pirate flag of Thomas Tew

OCEAN LEGENDS

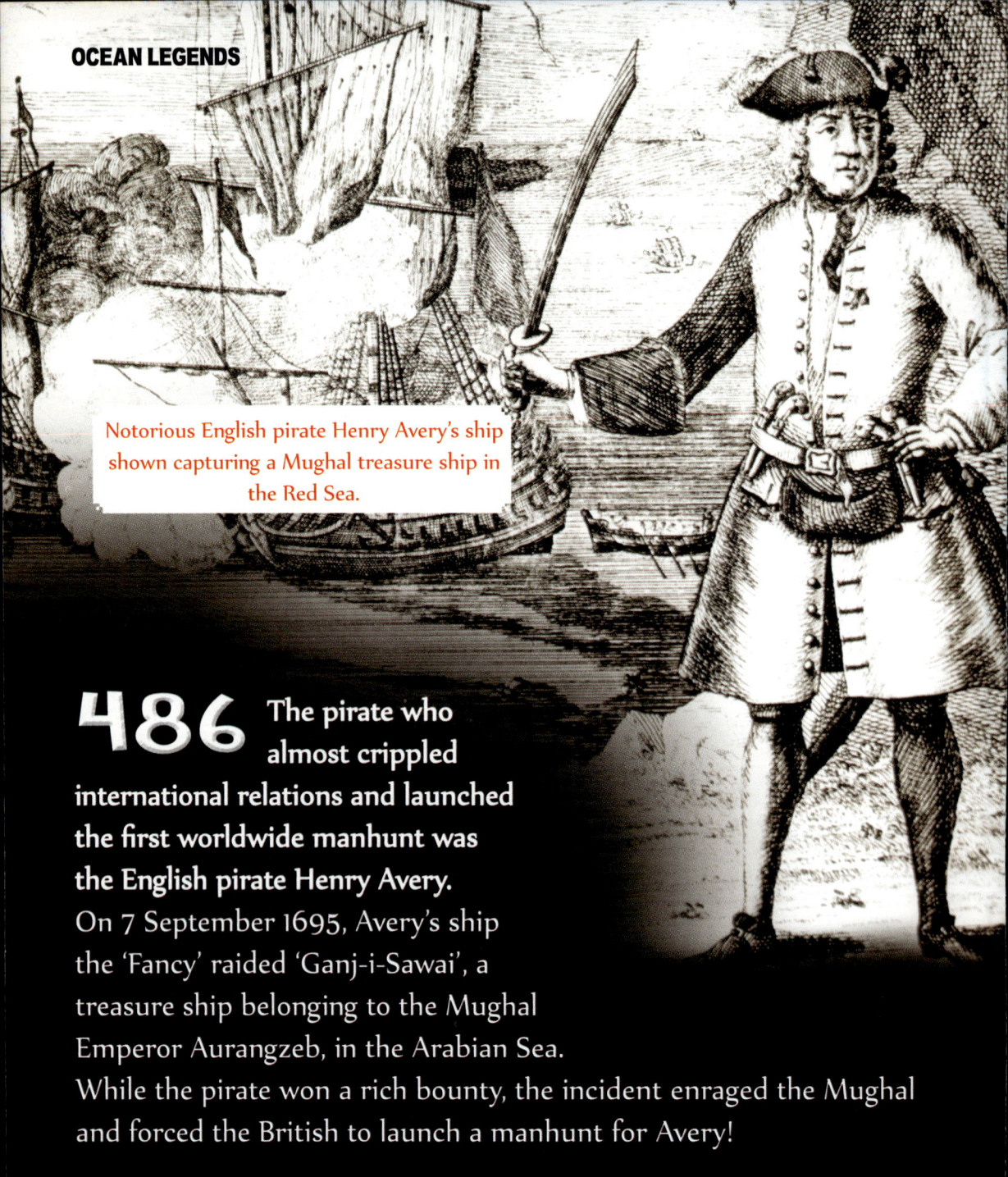

Notorious English pirate Henry Avery's ship shown capturing a Mughal treasure ship in the Red Sea.

486 **The pirate who almost crippled international relations and launched the first worldwide manhunt was the English pirate Henry Avery.** On 7 September 1695, Avery's ship the 'Fancy' raided 'Ganj-i-Sawai', a treasure ship belonging to the Mughal Emperor Aurangzeb, in the Arabian Sea. While the pirate won a rich bounty, the incident enraged the Mughal and forced the British to launch a manhunt for Avery!

487 **Bartholomew Roberts was forced to become a pirate, but he did a very good job of it!** Known as the fearsome 'Black Bart', he was one of the most successful pirates in the 'Golden Age of Piracy', during the 1700s. He was known for his cleverness and bravery, looting ships with almost no effort.

PIRATES AND FAMOUS LOOT

488 It was not only men who were pirates. Although, women were often considered too weak to become pirates, some women still made the ranks by disguising themselves as men. Two of the most famous women pirates were Anne Bonny and Mary Read, who operated during the Golden Age of Piracy. They were fearsome pirates, considered twice as ruthless as the men.

A stamp printed in Guinea shows Anne Bonny, an Irish woman and a famous pirate, in the series 'Transport- Ships & Pirates', issued in 2009.

Grace O'Malley's castle tower in Ireland.

489 Read and Bonny were neither the only women pirates, nor the most fearsome. The Chinese pirate Ching Shih, once led 80,000 pirates and 1,800 ships! During her exploits in early 1800s, her reputation in the seas around China was fearsome. Then, there was the Irish chieftain and pirate Grace O'Malley who preceded them all in the mid-1500s.

OCEAN LEGENDS

490 Some pirates fought political wars and became heroes. Sir Francis Drake, known as an explorer who led an expedition around the world, also doubled up as a pirate, raiding and looting Spanish ships. While the Spanish considered him a pirate, the British saw him as a hero who fought against their enemy the Spanish. He was awarded a knighthood in 1581 by Queen Elizabeth I.

Statue of Sir Francis Drake on Playmouth Hoe, in Devon, England.

491 Another pirate who became a heroic legend was Black Sam or Samuel Bellamy. Operating in the early 18th century, Bellamy was known for his kindness and charity. But it did not make him any less successful, as he captured over 53 ships! Today, his accumulated wealth would have amounted to around $120 million, making him the wealthiest pirate in recorded history.

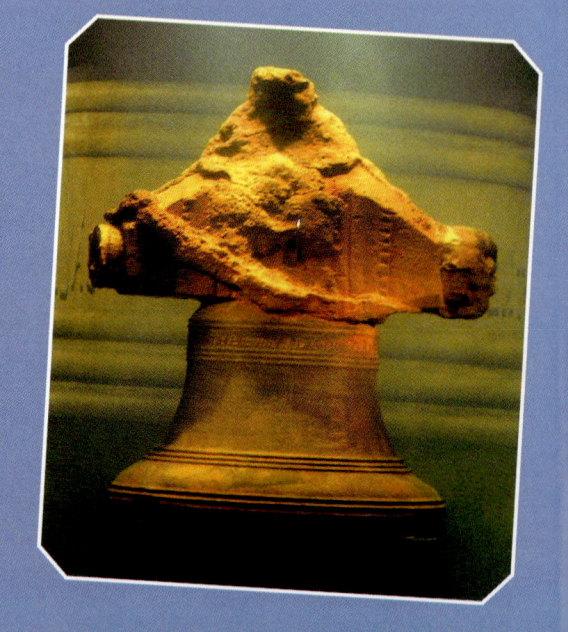

Tragedies and Myths

492 The oceans have given us some fantastic tales. Often, since people could not understand the reasons for phenomena on the seas, myths grew around it. For example, shipwrecks were often thought to be the work of the devil. In fact, some locations came to be seen as mysterious, dangerous and mythically powerful.

493 No other location in the world can equal the fearsome legend of the Bermuda Triangle. Located just off the coast of Bermuda, the legend started when a military plane and then its rescue party vanished at this location in 1945! But the truth is that many people cross this area every day without incident!

Ocean Legends

The Sargasso Sea in the North Atlantic Ocean.

494 **The Sargasso Sea has unique surface water currents, which give it many distinctive characteristics—clear deep blue water, a calm surface in contrast to the Atlantic Ocean, and an abundance of the sargassum seaweed.** Wind-powered sailboats would come to a standstill here and this gave rise to several legends, ranging from the attack of giant seaweed, to mysterious shipwrecks.

495 **Also called the Pacific Bermuda Triangle because of its location in the Pacific, just off the east coast of Japan, the Devil's Sea or the Dragon's Triangle is also associated with the disappearance of ships.** Sceptics have pointed out that the most prominent disappearance took place because of an underwater volcano, and all other disappearances were of small boats, which could have taken place for various reasons.

TRAGEDIES AND MYTHS

496 The ocean gives us many stories of shipwrecks. Of these, some are exaggerations and some are tragedies that are still remembered today. While the ocean was the most effective way to travel worldwide for the early explorers, it was often dangerous as well, with unexplained creatures, pirates and strange occurrences.

497 On 10 April 1912, a luxury British passenger liner sailed off from the port at Southampton in Britain. Considered the largest ship at that time, it was built as a luxury liner, offering a host of services and facilities that were unique at that time. It carried roughly 2,224 people in passengers and crew. This was the RMS Titanic.

Archival picture of the Titanic

OCEAN LEGENDS

Sinking of the ocean liner, the Titanic, witnessed by survivors in lifeboats.

498 **Early in the morning on 15 April 1912, the Titanic met with a tragedy.** It sank after colliding with an iceberg, and more than half its passengers died. This is still considered one of the deadliest maritime disasters during peacetime in modern history. The tragedy was worse, because several people died simply because of lack of lifeboats onboard. This later prompted the establishment of maritime safety rules.

499 **The wreck of the Titanic is almost as interesting as its voyage!** Lying at a depth of roughly 2.37 miles, the wreck was discovered in 1985. By now, it is home to many marine species, including metal-eating bacteria, which is slowly eroding the structure. It is estimated that the Titanic will soon disappear from the ocean floor!

500 **Some people try to find shipwrecks to loot them for the treasure they may have been carrying.** In particular, Spanish ships returning from the American colonies were known to carry a lot of silver which attracted many amateurs to find the wrecks. This is just one of the many, many legends that has become part of the folklore of the oceans!

The mythical and factual legends of the ocean.